GLOW UP yourself

CHELSEA CLARKE

ISBN: 978-1-0693824-1-2

Disclaimer

While the publisher has taken all reasonable steps to ensure that any website addresses mentioned in this book were accurate and accessible at the time of publication, neither the publisher nor the author assumes any responsibility for errors or for changes that occur for the availability, functionality, appropriateness, or ongoing relevance of any website, nor do they have any control over any third-party websites' content. Some names, locations, and identifying characteristics have been changed to protect the privacy of those depicted. Every effort has been made to identify and acknowledge trademarks within this book. The presence of any word, whether explicitly marked as a trademark or not, does not impact its legal status. All trademarks, registered trademarks, and product names mentioned herein are the property of their respective owners and are used only for identification or reference purposes. Their inclusion does not imply any affiliation, endorsement, or sponsorship. Additionally, the publisher has made efforts to trace copyright holders of any referenced materials. If any copyright-related oversight or omission is identified, please notify the publisher in writing, and appropriate corrections will be made in future editions or reprints.

The information contained in this book is provided for general informational and entertainment purposes only and may not be suitable for your situation. It is not legal, financial, tax, medical, or professional advice. Readers are encouraged to consult with a qualified professional before making any decisions related to legal matters, financial planning, investments, business, health, or any other personal or professional concerns. Neither the author nor the publisher assumes any responsibility for the accuracy, completeness, or applicability of the information presented and shall not be liable for any loss of profit or any other damages. By reading this book, you acknowledge and accept that you are solely responsible for your choices and actions.

BONUS RESOURCES

There is a bonus resource kit that pairs with this book. Inside, you'll find additional training, worksheets, and more. To get it for free, visit: https://GlowUpYourself.com/bonus/ or scan the QR code below.

Table of Contents

Introduction

If you've been a hot mess or an Olympic-level procrastinator, I've got awesome news for you. Today is a brand new day, sister. You do not have to stay stuck in a cycle of overthinking, underachieving, or undercharging any longer. I know you have waited long enough to take action on your goals. Maybe you're subconsciously hoping someone will show up and hand you your dream life or tell you, "Yes, you're allowed to want more. Go after the life you actually want." I have to break it to you: nobody's coming. And you don't need them to.

Because here's what you will do: you're going to *glow up yourself*. Yes, that's right. It's like saying "go fu*k yourself" to your old life, old mindset and giving a middle finger to every bad habit, self-doubt spiral, and excuse that's kept you small. Your life transformation isn't waiting for more time, more money, more followers, or more confidence. It's waiting for you to say, "I'm doing it anyway." But instead of "go fu*k yourself" (which is a negative, dead-end, low-vibe, loss-of-control kind of energy) I'm calling it "Glow Up Yourself." This puts a positive spin on your life overhaul, one that embraces the fact that you have all of the control.

By embodying Glow Up Yourself energy, you pave the way to your positive purpose, complete rebrand, and comeback tour. Do you want to start a business? Do it. Do you want to leave that soul-sucking job? Fire your boss. Do you want to reinvent yourself and embody the highest version of you there is? Consider it done.

However, this isn't a book about perfection. There are no boss babe clichés or bro marketing hustle culture stereotypes in here. It's about self-trust and action. The kind that builds momentum, wealth, and unshakable confidence. Truthfully, today is the day you stop treating success like some distant dream reserved for other people, and claim it for yourself.

Maybe you're fed up with watching others create their dream businesses. You keep looking for a sign from the universe, wondering when you'll break out, strike it big or go viral. You might have started a blog, brand, or side hustle. Still, it's not growing as you imagined. Now, you're questioning if you really have what it takes.

Or maybe you're already a six-plus-figure entrepreneur, and you're *exhausted*. Burned out from doing everything society told you to do, but still feeling behind. As if no matter what you do, you're always stuck playing catch-up. You've checked all the boxes and followed all the "rules," but where's the freedom? Where's the feeling of success? Why does it feel like no matter how much you do, you're never quite there?

Let me tell you this: *You are not the problem*. The system was never designed for women to thrive. It was built to keep us playing small, staying "nice," and waiting for permission. Screw that. *You do not need permission to create the life and business you want.*

That's why I wrote this book. To show you just how capable you really are.

You Already Have It

Most self-help books love to sell the idea that something is wrong with you. That you are inherently flawed, that you need to "fix" yourself. As if success is a far-off place, something to reach if you work hard enough. I strongly disagree. The truth is, your "best self" is not something outside of you, dangling in the future, waiting to be unlocked. It is not something you need to win, like a reward for good behavior.

At the end of *The Wizard of Oz*, Dorothy finds out she's worn the magic ruby slippers all along. The slippers that had the power to take her home. But, before Dorothy could actually use them, she had to go on a journey of learning to believe in her abilities and overcome her fears. Well, that's what we are doing here in this book. We will explore how to let go of what's not serving you, so you can align your brain, heart, and courage to achieve your wildest goals.

Your magic ruby slippers, aka your best self, already exists within you. She's simply been buried under layers of gunk. What kind of gunk, you ask? Oh, you know, just outdated expectations, societal conditioning, and every limiting belief given to you since birth. That's all!

Know that the question is not, "How do I become my best self?" The question is, "What do I need to let go of so I can finally express who I have always been?" *This* is the kind of glow up I am talking about.

So imagine for a moment, if your life were a movie, what would the audience be screaming at the screen, telling you to do right now? If you aren't sure yet, don't worry; this book will help you gain perspective outside of yourself. So that by the end of this read, you can see what the audience sees in you.

I've Been There

How do I know this? I know because, frankly, I've lived it. I founded my company, HerPaperRoute, from my couch. There was no master plan. No business degree. Just me, my laptop, and my newborn baby balanced on one arm while I typed with the other. I was broke as heck, a former waitress by night and marketing manager by day, and now on maternity leave with no savings.

Behind me, I had a highlight reel of bad decisions that could make even the worst reality TV star look wholesome. (Yes, you can bet I'll dish up all the embarrassing moments on my glow up journey in the pages that follow.) Having tried and failed at multiple business ideas before this, I spent years playing financial catch-up, simmering in self-doubt, and nursing more hangovers than business plans.

Eventually, something undeniable urged me to change. I was finally ready to rebrand myself and step into a new era. I was done waiting for someone to hand me an opportunity. So I made one. I started a blog simply because I felt a tiny spark of excitement about it. *Blogging felt fun.*

HerPaperRoute.com grew into a newsletter, a podcast, a membership, and a movement. A remarkable community of female entrepreneurs came together to support my mission. The mission: to help women profit from their ideas instead of overthinking them. Women who, like me, desired financial freedom, flexibility, and the chance to work from anywhere. Oh, and the confidence to say "no" to things that made our souls want to implode.

I didn't stop there! I started flipping websites. I fell in love with buying, scaling, and selling websites like high-value digital real estate. I became a website investor, and this little side quest led me to hit my business's most significant numbers yet. My audience got curious about website flipping, too. They asked me where to find a safe place to buy and sell websites. So, I founded a female-led acquisitions platform called Niche Investor, where creators and investors can safely buy and sell digital businesses.

As things expanded, there was a new challenge, a new fear, and a new version of myself that I had to face at each stage. Now, I get to help women start, scale, and exit their businesses, like the trailblazers they were born to be. No gatekeeping, fluff, or pretending success happens overnight. Just practical strategies, actions, and money moves.

I didn't glide into entrepreneurship on a perfectly curated career path. I bootstrapped, finessed, and stumbled my way into building a multi-figure digital business purely out of survival. I have skills, sure, but let's be real: my ADHD, misophonia, and a deep aversion to soul-sucking office culture make me wildly unemployable. Yet, I love working for myself, from home, where no one can micromanage me or force me into pointless meetings.

When I finally realized I could replace my salary with an online business, and I'd never have to clock in at a "real" job again, *everything shifted.* This was the light bulb moment that took me way too long to figure out. Trust me; I wish someone had sucker-punched me with it sooner. I didn't have this realization until I was thirty. THIRTY! *That's 168 in dog years!*

It's Never Too Late

Before that, I was convinced I had already messed up my life too much to ever really turn things around. But here's the thing: rock bottom is not a vacant pit. It's a launchpad. One that is ready to hurl your cute butt into your new reality. A reality that YOU get to design and call into existence. If I can glow up my entire life, so can you.

I don't want you spending years overthinking, doubting yourself, or waiting for the "perfect moment" like I did. I understand if you feel left behind or think you've wasted time. I've been there. Drinking too much, making bad decisions, working jobs that sucked my soul dry, and staying in bad relationships too long. If your past seems too messy for the future you want, you're not alone. But you are not too late. You are not too old. You're not one bad day away from selling feet pics!

No more overthinking. No more "I'll do it later." No more romanticizing procrastination. This book presents a step-by-step, no-fluff, micro-habit-driven strategy to get you from idea to launch. Without the overwhelm, the self-sabotage, or the urge to set your laptop on fire whenever you think about starting.

So, if you've found yourself on the rock-bottom launchpad (or feeling like you could find yourself there any day now), congrats! There's only one direction to go from here. Will you make the decision that you want a better situation? By holding this book in your hands, you've already decided you do. Yay you!

About This Book

Glow Up Yourself is about what you can do to step into the best version of yourself. It is your no-BS guide to leveling up your life, your money, and your confidence—and to finally do the thing that's been rattling around in your brain for so long. It's about your new life glow up. This isn't some stuffy, corporate business book that tells you to hustle harder and manifest your way to success, and I am not a guru.

You already have every ability within you to hijack your free will *now* so that you can start living your best life. I'm just here to provide you with some daily habits and simple strategies to get you in the zone. If you feel like something is missing or that you're meant for more, good.

But I have to warn you. No one is coming to wake you up early, hand you the perfect business plan, force you to exercise, do your shadow work, or sprinkle magic dust on your half-baked ideas to turn them into a multi-figure empire. Unfortunately, there is no business fairy godmother, no motivational pixie, no secret club of rich people dying to hand over their money because you seem nice.

Girl, no one is going to glow you up for you; you have to *glow up yourself*. And YES, you can do it. This book is going to give you some much-needed butt-kickery and arm you with some of the best healthy habits I know to get you in the flow. Sound cool? Let's get to work.

Who This Book Is For

» This book is for the woman who knows she's meant for more. It's for the over thinkers, perfectionists, and "I'll start when I'm ready" types. The ones who have spent years watching other people build the life and business they want while telling themselves, "One day, I'll do it too." It's for anyone who doubts herself, feels stuck, or lacks inspiration. It's for those wondering if they are making a meaningful contribution to the world.

» This book is also for the woman who thinks she's already screwed up her one shot at success. The woman who has made questionable life choices. Perhaps having put a few too many dents in her reputation at a few too many office parties or hit rock bottom so hard she practically owns a timeshare there. Whose life choices read like a personality quiz titled 'Which Bad Idea Are You?' If you've ever thought, "I've made too many mistakes to turn this around," you're wrong. This book is here to slap that lie right out of your head and help you build something wildly successful. Mistakes, regrets, and all.

» It's for the 20-something who feels like everyone else is five steps ahead while she's still trying to figure out how to pretend she has it together. The one watching LinkedIn promotions roll in for her college classmates while she's sitting there wondering if she can put 'managed multiple crisis situations' (aka her own life) on her résumé.

» It's for the 40-plus woman who's questioning every decision she's ever made. The one wondering if it's too late to start over, switch careers, and finally do the thing she's been putting off for years.

» It's for the woman who dreams of firing her boss and being financially independent, with the ability to explore the world on a whim. Even though currently her only travel plans consist of going to the mountains to scream.

» It's for the woman with ADHD who dances between days of feeling like "I have so many ideas, and I can do everything, all at once!" to "My brain is completely empty, and I can't focus on or accomplish even putting my laundry away without having a breakdown." If your mental to-do list looks like a chaotic crime scene and you thrive on the adrenaline of last-minute panic, congratulations! This book is practically custom-built for you.

» It's for the divorcee who wants to reinvent herself, the woman staring at her reflection thinking, "Well, now what?" (And when did these chin hairs get so much personality?) The woman who has spent years pouring into someone else's dreams, someone else's life, and now? It's YOUR turn.

You are not broken. You are not behind. You are not out of time. You just need a good strategy and a push in the right direction. And this book, well, consider it your GPS. If you're here, it means you're done settling. You're done playing the supporting role in someone else's success story. I'm already so proud of you.

Mantra: *I do not care how many times I have to start over. I am not settling for a life I don't want.*

Quick note to the men reading this: Yes, this book was written by a woman, for women. But if you're a man flipping through these pages, welcome. You're invited to stay. Just know, some of the topics we cover might make you uncomfortable. They might challenge you to consider the way you show up for the women in your life. Cool with that? Good. Stick around.

Bonus Resources

Head over to GlowUpYourself.com/bonus to get free access to the bonus materials and extra training linked to this book.

1

Wanting It

Right now, your mind is doing mental gymnastics as you wonder, "Should I start a business?" "Should I quit my job?" "Should I ask for a raise?" "Should I fake my own death?" I'm going to tell you to stop "should-ing" all over yourself. It's time to put pen to paper and map out a plan for what you really WANT. Because when you know what you want, there's no question about what you should do. Your internal GPS simply guides you to everything you need to achieve or receive it.

Trouble is, many women have been conditioned not to have wants or not to believe in their wants. We're taught to be selfless. That ambition is "greedy." To not ask too much, be too ambitious, and definitely not take up too much space. We're conditioned to make ourselves useful, not be demanding, and to be grateful for whatever scraps of success we can get.

And so, we hesitate. We second-guess. We tell ourselves we might not need that raise, that big chance, or that dream business. We convince ourselves that we don't deserve that soft life where we don't have to be in survival mode 24/7. We downplay our goals and shrink ourselves. Sometimes, we even apologize for having dreams in the first place. Ugh, why?

Because we've been trained to believe that wanting more is selfish. As in, choosing to stay single and child-free is "selfish" (yet, if we have "too many" kids, we are also selfish). That confidence is cocky, and assertiveness is bitchy.

Meanwhile, men are out there confidently asking for promotions, even when they aren't qualified. They are raising their rates without a second thought. They are launching businesses with zero hesitation, no matter their experience.

So, here's the truth: Your desires are not unreasonable. Your goals are not "too big." You do not need anyone's approval to want what you want. The only thing standing between you and the life you actually want is the belief that you don't deserve it. Spoiler alert! You do. We all do!

Money gives you options, power, and freedom. I believe that every woman who wishes it can be wealthy, financially independent and with the freedom to do as she pleases. The kind of woman who never has to ask *anyone* for permission. You can be that woman. And it starts today by claiming your wants. Right now, grab a piece of paper and make a list of every single thing you want. And I mean everything. Big, tiny, wild, ridiculous... nothing is off-limits.

The only rules:

- No self-policing.
- No "That's too expensive."

- No "That's too big."
- No "That's too hard."
- No "That's too greedy."

Write it all down. The dream house, business, client, body, book deal, or brand partnership. The luxurious skincare routine, the paid-off debt. Being able to take a damn nap at any time of the day without guilt. Let it all hit the page unfiltered. When you stop editing your desires before they even make it out of your brain, you start to see what's actually festering under the surface: what you really want when you're brutally honest with yourself. And more importantly, are you finally ready to stop pretending you don't want more?

Think about it. As a child, you didn't doubt your worth. You didn't worry about being good enough or if you deserved to take up space. You didn't think your dreams were too big. *That came later.* For years, you absorbed messages telling you to play small, be realistic, fit in, stay quiet, and stop wanting so much.

Here's the thing. That powerful, unfiltered, unafraid version of you? She's still there. She's not waiting for success to find her, not hoping to become worthy one day. She is simply waiting for you to strip away the layers that have convinced you she doesn't exist. Self-improvement is not about becoming someone new. It's about removing everything that is not you. It's about unlearning, letting go, and remembering what's always been within you.

In fact, my goal is to help you slash the timeline from dream to reality in half (or more) and get you to take action so you start your life glow-up NOW. I hope that by the time you turn the last page of this book, you'll feel lighter, bolder, and utterly unapologetic about taking up space. That you'll stop overthinking and start taking action. That you'll finally see yourself as you are, someone who is capable, brilliant, and 100% worthy of success.

The only difference between you and the people out there living *your dream* is that 1) they started, and 2) they didn't give up when it got sucky. That's it. So take a deep breath. Let go of the doubt. You're exactly where you need to be.

Double Double

I was standing in a Tim Hortons coffee spot on the side of the highway in Cowichan, BC, Canada, the moment I lost $400,000 USD (or $560,000 in Canadian currency). Staring at my phone in disbelief, my eyes blurry as I read the words: "We've decided we will not be acquiring your company. We wish you the best."

Up until that moment, I thought the deal was a sure thing. I had met with the potential buyers on Zoom calls for weeks, assisting in their due diligence. The terms of the sale agreement were all worked out. They had seemed so excited to acquire my company. I really thought I was going to be free to move on from the business I so desperately wanted to exit.

Then, just like that, with one measly email, they were out. The sale was canceled. The SIX FIGURES I thought I had in the bag went poof, gone, ciao baby. My mind raced as I thought back to the weeks of Zoom meetings I'd had with them. What did I do? What did I say? Did I weird them out? I f*cked up the deal, I thought to myself gravely.

I would learn later, through doing some much-needed shadow work, that in life, it is not possible to f*ck up what's meant for you. And that when a deal fails, it was not meant to close from the start. You were meant to have the experience of dealing with the counterparty, but not to sell to them. The right buyer is going to be around the corner soon enough.

Remember this piece of advice because it will guide you through many would-be heartaches as a business owner. What is meant for you will never pass you by because the universe always has your back. Everything, and I mean everything, is always working out in your favor.

> The universe only has three answers for you: yes, not yet, and I have something better for you.

I would later learn that this rejection would be just one of many. Over the next three years, I would face many more nos as I searched for the right buyer for my startup. With each almost sale that ended in another buyer backing out, I started to care less and less. With each no, I felt less attached to any emotion, to the point that I didn't even care if I ever sold it. Yep, I'm just out here taking blows and smiling as I deadpan repeat, "I respect your decision, thank you," as each door slammed in my face. "It's for the best, I'm sure," I'd assure myself again. By the tenth time it happened, I did not care in the slightest and felt absolutely nothing when I was told the sale was a no. In fact, I stopped feeling like I was trying to sell a business; rather, I just took it as more practice in rejection therapy!

With each "no," I felt less and less attached to any emotion, to the point that I didn't even care if I ever sold it. Yep, I'm just out here taking blows and smiling as I deadpan repeat, "I respect your decision, thank you," as each door slammed in my face. "It's for the best, I'm sure," I'd assure myself again. But all that 'emotionless energy' would come with time, later. Because in this *particular* moment as I stood outside of the Tim Hortons, watching as $560,000 evaporated from my grasp, such comprehension of losing it being for my greater good was lost on me. I was mad, honey.

What I didn't know then was that right around the corner, I was about to sign a client for the business's biggest project yet. A project that would pay such a significant fee that it made me reconsider selling entirely. Not only that, but the revenue ultimately generated from that one client brought the valuation of my business up *remarkably*. So not only would I have missed out on that client if I'd sold the company to any of those "rejection therapy" people, but also on how my business ended up being worth far more than before.

Not long ago, I couldn't even imagine having a business worth half a million dollars, let alone coming so close to cashing in on it. The idea that someone would offer me $560,000 for something I had built? Unthinkable. But that's the power of owning digital businesses: You create something once, grow it, and it becomes a valuable, *sellable* asset.

Let's rewind for a second. Before I became a website investor, before I owned multiple revenue-earning websites, I was a broke university student. I had no idea that flipping online businesses was possible. I was just trying to figure out how to afford groceries, let alone a future.

It's been a wild transformation, and I want you to know I didn't start with an advantage. I began with zero funds, lots of self-doubt, and the very real pressure of not wanting to struggle forever. And that's why I believe owning a digital business is so valuable, even if it takes a while. The emotional roller coaster of being an online entrepreneur is real. Yet, it is so worth it because that's how you buy back your freedom.

So, let's go back to the beginning. Before the six-figure valuations, before the exit strategies, before "glowing up" was even a thing.

Be Your Own Sugar Daddy

Way back in 2004, I was sitting in my university cafeteria, as I usually did in between classes. I couldn't afford to actually eat there, but I'd often sit there and read the paper or shoot the shit with my friend, Jane. That day, I was doing both. Jane and I were flipping through the paper, skimming the public interest pieces and giggling at the scandalous ads on the back page.

I was nineteen and in a particularly tough period in my life. I was struggling to pay my rent, tuition, and all the other expenses that come with being alive. My after-school job waiting tables was not bringing in enough cash, and frankly, the cost of my rent was becoming unmanageable. I wasn't sure if I'd be able to come up with enough money to pay for next semester's tuition.

All around me were students who seemed to exist on a different planet entirely. A parent or a family trust fund was paying their tuition, and they never had to worry about making rent for their apartments. They drove to school in cars while I walked, rain or shine. *Womp womp.* Honestly, I *wanted* to be the bigger person and not let all that get to me. But the truth? I was jealous, for real.

Meanwhile, barely scraping by, I was more than a little butthurt that I couldn't come up with the $200 to buy a textbook for my art history class. Yet there I was, working at a restaurant where the price of one menu item was my entire week's grocery budget, smiling, nodding, and passionately recommending dishes I had never tasted in my life. "Oh, the truffle risotto? Exquisite." "The steak? Melt-in-your-mouth perfection." I mean, it probably wasn't a lie if you liked steak and you weren't a vegetarian like me. I had no clue what the food there tasted like, personally. I was simply a master at regurgitating Yelp reviews. On second thought, I did know what a *few* menu items tasted like, but only because I was no stranger to scarfing down plates of food that customers sent back to the kitchen if something was made "wrong"! Stop judging me!

Watching my peers seemingly breeze through life while their parents covered rent, tuition, and "just because" spending money for them felt like a personal slap in the face to me. PLEASE. Well, the resentment wasn't just a passing thought anymore. It was settling in, stacking up like storm clouds, slowly morphing into something heavier, something dangerously close to full-blown depression.

"Look at page twenty. A girl makes $7,000 a month as a...a sugar baby?" Jane squinted at the page.

"What's that?" I asked. This was the first time I'd heard the term sugar baby. I flipped to page twenty to see the article.

It was new to Jane, too. She scanned the article and said with a smile, "Some guy pays her for...you know, like an escort. Except, like, they go on dates and trips; it's not just a secret roadside motel thing. He's her 'sugar daddy.'"

"Good for her," I sighed, knowing full well that no matter how tempting that sounded right about then, I could never do something like that. Just like how I couldn't be a stripper. As much as I respect women for doing as they please in their own lives, my fear of disappointing my mom stopped me from pursuing such occupations.

I stared at the words on the paper: "*Seven thousand dollars a month.*" By contrast, I wasn't even pulling in $1,200 a month at my waitressing job, and my rent alone was $950. Starving was not appealing, but the thought of dealing with sugar daddies was even less so.

"I'll keep that option on the back burner!" Jane laughed, flipping the page. "Oh look, you can sell your eggs to Americans..."

I shot her a look.

She continued, "Or maybe marry a rich dude?"

I dropped my face into my palms. "Jane, I want to *be* the rich dude. I want to be my *own* sugar daddy!"

That was my watershed moment. A declaration to the universe that I wanted something different for my life than the status quo. Although, at nineteen, it felt like nothing more than an unfounded wish. I had no idea it could actually happen. See, I knew that I wanted to be in control of my life, to get myself into a good situation financially and on my own terms. I didn't want to be a waitress or a broke art student forever.

Yet back then, I had no idea how or what to do to get on the right track. I didn't know where to look for advice. Nor did I have any mentors. It was before Instagram, YouTube, Facebook, TikTok, or Pinterest existed. No one was online, showing regular people like me what was possible yet. At that moment, I felt at a total loss, in total despair.

Looking back, it was a significant turning point because it was when I realized I wanted more for myself than my current reality. Even though I wasn't sure what that could look like yet. Although things felt hopeless then, at least I knew that subjecting myself to the dominance of a man *was not it.*

Despite it all, I did manage to graduate. In a *hilarious* turn of events, I (along with every other new grad) walked off stage at our graduation ceremonies and into the absolute dumpster fire that was the 2008 job market. We entered the real world that year, bright-eyed, degrees in hand, ready to land a great job. Only for the Global Financial Crisis to say, "Ha ha, nope!" The economy had just imploded, and suddenly, all those promises about how a degree would open doors? Yeah, no, those doors were locked, barricaded, and had giant "WE'RE NOT HIRING, GO AWAY" signs slapped on them.

Job listings were scarce, and rejections plenty. The companies that were hiring were paying less, slashing benefits, and treating job seekers like we should be grateful for their lowball offers. The cushy hiring bonuses, decent salaries, and stable career paths people had before the crash? Gone. I wasn't just struggling to get ahead; I was struggling even to get started. This first experience of the real world was probably one of the things that radicalized me. The traditional job market wasn't going to work for me. I was going to have to build something of my own.

That moment chatting with Jane in our university cafeteria was two decades ago. And since then, social media has certainly come around. Access to technology, information, and digital publishing has skyrocketed. Right now, this very moment is the best time in history to own a digital business. No, that's not an exaggeration; it's a fact. The barriers to entry have never been lower, while the opportunities have never been more abundant.

The Internet is basically handing you a golden ticket to build your empire from your couch. Think about it. Only a decade ago, launching a business meant dealing with leases, warehouses, and inventory nightmares. And let's not forget cold-calling strangers while sweating through a blazer, ew.

Now? You can build a brand, market a product, and make money all from your laptop or phone without ever leaving your house. If you have WiFi, a good idea, and the audacity to start, you're already ahead of 90% of people.

Since I sat in that cafeteria feeling like my future was a black hole, a hopeless, lost cause, I've built and sold multiple digital businesses that hit valuations of six figures and then seven in the creator economy. I've built a community of thousands of fierce women creators around my brand.

So if you're feeling lost, stuck, or like success is reserved for people with trust funds or at least, matching socks, trust me, I've been there. And if I can build something from nothing, you sure as hell can, too. Even if you're currently broke, nineteen, ninety, uneducated, uncertain, or unprepared, you can absolutely glow up your whole life and be your own sugar daddy.

The E Word

Most non-entrepreneurial people tend to get weird around the word *entrepreneur*. You'll notice the odd looks your friends give you when you first announce that you have started a business. It's as though you just announced that you're giving up modern medicine to treat yourself exclusively with moon water and interpretive dance. Even you will probably notice an uneasy feeling in your stomach the first time you say, "I'm an entrepreneur," out loud.

Take it from me; you might still feel it the 10,000th time you say it. And, honestly, saying you're an entrepreneur produces a buttload of assumptions and expectations. Some people will think it means you're trying to be a big shot now, and then they'll judge you for not looking or behaving the way they expect: "You're an entrepreneur? Oh, I haven't heard of that company." "What ranking were you given in *Forbes* this year?" "I don't see your company on the stock exchange. You aren't publicly traded?" "When did you do a TED Talk exactly?" "I've never seen you on the cover of a magazine." "I don't see Oprah in your phone contacts."

In other words, people only seem to think in terms of the prominent CEOs in the big headlines. You might worry that others won't see you as a "real" entrepreneur if you're not in the spotlight. The truth is that all that media attention and PR has nothing to do with *being* an entrepreneur; those are just some possible *results* that can come from the job. If that's even your goal. For most of us, strutting across a stage or posing for the cover of Forbes magazine is not the goal.

So, what is an entrepreneur, really? When explaining to SpongeBob what a local salesfish's job is, Squidward said it best: "He's an entrepreneur. *He sells things to people.*" That's it. Entrepreneurs sell things to people. Release yourself from all the other junk, achievements, statistics, and expectations people may or may not have for you. If you sell things, you're an entrepreneur.

When I started my company in 2017, I had to face the word *entrepreneur* for the first time. It seemed like such a big fancy word for what I was actually doing day-to-day (which was writing content from my couch in cozy PJs while breastfeeding!) How can I be an entrepreneur when that's how I'm spending my day? No board meetings, no power suits, no *synergizing efficiencies for shareholders*. Yet, my new blogging business was generating more money than any salary I had ever made at a "real" job. So, yes, I had to accept that an entrepreneur could look like me, cozy pj's and all.

Entrepreneurship is simple: You have something to offer, and you sell it to people. That's it. You don't need to overcomplicate it, make it fancy, or wait until you feel "official" (because, surprise, that moment never magically arrives). You know what makes you a real entrepreneur? Selling something. Period. You could be making $5 or $500,000; it doesn't matter. If you're out there offering a product, service, or idea that people are buying, congratulations, you are doing the thing.

Also, and this might surprise some people, you don't need fancy branding, an expensive website, or an LLC before you even make your first dollar. You don't even need a power suit, babe. Those things are optional and can come into play later. But right out of the gate, you only need to launch with the most straightforward, most efficient tools. Not the fanciest or *expensive-iest!*

And guess what? You are not a failure if you aren't hosting summits, scaling at warp speed, or "disrupting the industry." Sure, these are all things you can do if you want to. But those things aren't the *point*. The point is to make money doing something you love and to build a life on your terms. That's it.

So, let's release the unnecessary pressure and the weird guilt, shall we? You don't have to "prove" your entrepreneurship to anyone. You just have to start selling, keep learning, and figure it out as you go. That's the entire game. Seriously, stop overthinking and go make an offer. Don't worry; I'm here to walk you through the process of creating your offer coming up in this book. Just know that *selling* is what makes you an entrepreneur. Not some ridiculous LinkedIn title or an ego-inflating milestone that doesn't actually pay the bills.

Why Now

I bet this isn't the first time you've considered a) starting a new business or b) taking your business to the next level. The biggest threat to your success? Waiting. Right now, someone with half your talent is making money online because they took action while you were overthinking it. You don't need the perfect idea, perfect website, or perfect timing. The Internet rewards speed and consistency, not perfection.

You just need to start. The creator economy is exploding, and every day you wait is a day that you could have been earning. The best time to start a business is today. The best time to launch a new product is today. The best time to buy a blog (aka a revenue-generating asset) is, you guessed it, today!

Need more proof? Well, for starters, it's never been this low-cost and low-risk to become a business owner. There's no storefront, no expensive overhead, and no begging banks for a loan. Someone can start with basically zero dollars and scale from there. People are addicted to online shopping and digital content. Whether it's products, coaching, templates, courses, or even Etsy shops, people spend more time and money online than ever. So, be where the money is. Create something that serves a need to offer buyers and put it in front of them. (More on that in Chapter 2, keep reading.)

No kidding, think of how easy it is to publish something and conduct business on the Internet nowadays. We are spoiled. Geez, I remember the day I first met the Internet. Growing up, I spent much of my childhood at my grandparents' house in West Vancouver. As a little kid, I thought it was so cool how my grandpa, Roy Peterson, an editorial cartoonist, got to work from home, drawing. Grandpa gained some fame in Canada. He won the National Newspaper Award seven times, more than any other journalist or cartoonist in his lifetime. He was also a recipient of the Order of Canada. The Governor General's official statement was, "Roy Peterson is one of our finest editorial cartoonists. Expertly blending humour and satire, he has provided insightful commentary on our political landscape."

My grandma, on the other hand, ran the entire business behind his brand. She was the bookkeeper, the runner, the executive assistant, the CEO, COO, CFO, CMO, and everything else. While also raising five kids, being the house manager, personal chef, seamstress, and maid. Oh, and the babysitter of me, ugh!

I'd often tag along with her to the *Vancouver Sun* building downtown as she hand-delivered Grandpa's cartoon for the newspaper each week. Driving in her black Mustang, Grandpa's cartoon would be carefully balanced on my lap. It was always drawn in ink on heavy poster board. On one trip, someone at the *Vancouver Sun* wanted to show us a computer. Probably to try to help Grandma out, to save her the weekly drive downtown. "You know we can accept emails now," he declared, pointing to a small gray computer.

I was familiar with computers from my school's computer lab, but there, only to insert a floppy disk to play *Oregon Trail*. "What's email?" I asked, staring at the colorful little window box on the screensaver.

"It's *revolutionary!*" he beamed excitedly, jazz hands waving, "With this new system, Windows 95, the world as we know it is about to change forever. Watch this!" He then walked us through the process of sending an email. I was in awe. You could type something on one computer, and then someone on a different computer could read it, like magic. I don't think Grandma was too impressed. How was she supposed to squish the poster board into a computer?!

A few months later, I created my first email address at school. We didn't have a computer at home, and I didn't know what else you could do with them other than look up *Sailor Moon* lore. They cut out so much quality backstory during the English translation! The Internet revealed it all! It's funny to realize how far technology has come.

Think about how lucky we are nowadays to have AI and automation, too. AI can literally do most of the work for you. You don't need a full-time staff when tools that can automate sales, marketing, and customer service exist. Another reason why now is the time to own a digital business (and it's a biggie) is social media! Social media is your free advertising platform, something marketers could only have dreamed about a few decades ago. Nowadays, you don't need a marketing degree or a Super Bowl commercial–level budget; you just need to know how to create content that stops the scroll.

But what about financial uncertainty? What about the risk of not having an employer, Chelsea? Ah, yes, the illusion of security that comes with a paycheck. Let's be so for real: as an employee your income is capped. Also, your financial future rests in the hands of people who would replace you in a heartbeat if it saved the company a few dollars. Where is the security in that? Now, let's discuss what happens when you own an income stream.

1. **No one gets to cap your income, except you**. When you work for someone else, you're trading your time for money at a fixed rate. Promotions? A slow, frustrating climb. Raises? A couple of extra dollars a year, if you're lucky. Yet, in your own business, there is no cap. You decide what you earn, set your prices, and scale on your terms. When you hit your next financial goal, there's no

awkward meeting with a boss as you beg for a raise. As an owner, you just give yourself one.

2. **You have full control over your life.**Digital businesses give women something that traditional jobs never will: total autonomy. Want to launch a new offer, pivot your strategy, or change things up? No boardroom meetings, no red tape, just action. Want to take a vacation? Go ahead anytime. You don't have to submit a request, hoping your boss will approve it. Heck, as your own boss, you don't even have to ask for a day off to go to a doctor's appointment. Seriously, how embarrassing is it to have to ask your employer for permission to see your doctor?!

3. **You get to earn from multiple income streams.**A job gives you one paycheck. Usually, if that job disappears, so does your entire income. With a digital business, you can scale and diversify as you wish, so you're never dependent on just one income source. You have options, such as freelancing, courses, memberships, affiliate income, coaching, you name it.

4. **Most importantly, you can create passive income**, which pays you even when you're sleeping, sick, or on vacation. Multiple income streams can be critical during times of economic downturns. Note, however, that recessions and economic shifts actually favor digital businesses. During downturns, traditional companies experiencing unpredictable demand are still stuck with high

overhead and other costs, while online entrepreneurs can much more easily pivot, adapt, and make money from anywhere.

5. **The future of work is digital**. Thanks to the Internet and AI, digital and remote work provide a great alternative to traditional, in-office jobs, especially for women. We can run our businesses from anywhere (hello, home office in pj's or a cozy café) and reach customers all over the world with no commute. We can create our schedules, fitting work around school pickup and making wellness a priority. All that flexibility seriously pays off in mental health. A study at the U.S. Career Institute found that 48% of people feel less stressed when they work from home. Less stress, more freedom? Sign me up! Finally, the digital economy is leveling the playing field *for once* (*about damn time*). It doesn't care about your gender, your résumé, your degree, or who you know. Instead, it rewards action, innovation, and consistency. All things that you can control.

6. **It's a way to build long-term wealth**.A job will pay your bills, but it doesn't build wealth. A digital business, in contrast, is real financial power. Instead of working for a paycheck, you're creating an asset. As an asset grows in value, it gives you freedom and helps you break free from financial dependence. When you own a digital asset, such as a website that earns money, you have something

> valuable to sell later. Did you know that a website earning $1,000 a month can sell for around $40,000? Yes! I've sold and brokered the sale of thousands of websites over the years for both myself and my clients. That valuation amount for such earnings is not unusual.

So, what's really riskier? Betting on yourself or betting on a corporate system designed to keep you stuck? As your own boss, you gain the ability to own your time, your income, and your future. What's more, you have endless access to information, tech, and convenience. All things that generations before us couldn't even fathom.

As a wide-eyed kid meeting the Internet in the '90s, I had no idea where the World Wide Web would take me. Or any of us. Yet, thanks to it, I feel so fortunate to exist at this time in history. Our grandparents had to work outrageously hard to build their businesses and make art without the Internet. Now, we can do it all with just a few taps. Since you and I are so immensely privileged to be alive in this digital age, where things can be so easy, don't make it harder for yourself than it is. Only ask yourself: why not now?

Decisions

If you want to be an entrepreneur, then the first thing you need to do is *decide* to own a business. Usually, that decision pairs with choosing to have a better life. Yay, you! It's time to glow up. Once you've made that verdict, opportunities to make new decisions every day from here on are unlocked. First will be choices about things your brain probably never had to consider before, like deciding on a niche, an audience, a platform, and something to sell. And, you'll contemplate, probably for too long, whether you can afford to hire people to help you scale.

As your life glows up, your consciousness will expand. Now, you'll find yourself deciding to quit toxic friends and toxic habits. You'll fall in love with bettering yourself. With your own business, yes, you will experience new types of stress, and many times, making decisions will be difficult. It may be especially tough when you have to fire an employee or contractor. Yet, being able to make those calls is crucial. Throughout the ups and downs, each new step keeps you going.

When I was fifteen, I had a three-week courtship with a boy from my school; let's call him Aaron. He wasn't kind, funny, good-looking, or interesting, and our personalities did not vibe, so I have no idea why we were hanging out, even if it was just a short stint. Regardless, I'll never forget it. One day, we walked to the ice cream shop between classes. At the counter, standing in front of the register, he asked, "What do you want?"

"I don't know," I shrugged. "Maybe chocolate brownie, maybe mint chip." I hadn't decided yet. And I didn't really care. Either would be good.

"Pick one," he urged, visibly annoyed for some reason.

"I don't know," I shrugged again.

Rolling his eyes, he exclaimed, "Ugh! You're so indecisive!"

This word seeped into my skin. Indecisive? Am I indecisive, really? Is that a trait I have as a person? It's funny the things we pack so quickly into our personhood during our young years. This word would stick with me later, throughout my twenties, as I wondered what I wanted to do with my life. When I struggled, I would remember that moment in the ice cream shop. I'd question if Aaron was right about me and that word. I'm indecisive. I can't make decisions.

A few years later, that chatter in my brain would be cured so that what Aaron said would never perplex me again. It was a sunny August afternoon, and I was skipping work with Jane. We had decided to have "sick days" from work and had called in to our respective office jobs, feigning illness. For us, a sick day was when we'd do sick things all day, like chill at the beach and go to the movies. On this particular sick day, we were at the skate park drinking wine concealed in coffee cups. She was retelling a conversation she had had with a guy at work who called her indecisive. Her response to him was, "I'm not indecisive; I'm indifferent."

Oooooh. I'm not indecisive. I'm indifferent. YES. How empowering is that? And true. It's not that we can't choose; it's that often neither of the options is important enough to us to waste attention on. If only I could have had that clapback in the ice cream shop at fifteen!

Life lessons: 1) We are great at making decisions when the decision matters, and 2) no one has the power to assign negative personality traits to us.

Indifference is pretty powerful. It might even be the real secret to happiness. Not in a "meh, nothing matters" way, but in a powerful, unbothered "either way, I win" kind of way. It's a type of neutrality that means: If it happens, great. If it doesn't, also great. Come what may, I'm good. That's where true freedom lies. It's when you're not grasping at an outcome so tightly that you strangle the joy right out of it and when you stop begging, forcing, or over-attaching yourself to what must happen in order for you to be okay.

The universe (and, let's be honest, people) can smell desperation. Whether it's sales, love, or money, the energy of "I need this to work, or I will combust into a tragic heap of unworthiness" is not the energy of a winner. The energy of a winner is, "I would love for this to happen, but I don't need it to happen."

Stay cool. Stay content and roll with the punches, pivot when needed, and trust that whatever happens next is exactly as it's supposed to be. Be excited but not attached. Be hopeful but not desperate. Be open to the best-case scenario but unbothered if it takes a detour. Because when outcomes aren't a big deal, you don't waste energy worrying about them, and you've stopped gripping the steering wheel in white-knuckled panic, that's when life starts moving in your favor.

That said, in some cases, being indifferent doesn't always serve you. As a business owner specifically, you will need to be able to make decisions that matter. Yes, you will need to have an opinion, take a side, and make small and large decisions constantly. On the daily, you'll have to decide to keep trying, keep creating, keep taking chances, and keep believing in your dream.

That's because, usually, you are the only person there to keep the dream alive. You have to wake up each morning and decide to put in the effort to find the money. That's right! You have to *find the money* now and every day. You must seek out possibilities for income at every opportunity. Are you open to seeing them?

Of course, if you haven't started your business yet, but it's a goal, then the only decision you need to focus on right now is the decision to become a business owner. Once you decide that, yes, you do want to step into that role, then you'll move on to decisions like: What will you sell? Who do you want to sell to?

The best part about building your own business is that you get to set the rules. You get to decide how much you work, how much you earn, and what success looks like. No waiting for a green light from external sources. No relying on someone else's opinion or income. None of the "let-me-check-with-my-husband-before-I-make-a-financial-decision" energy. When you build something that belongs to you, and your success isn't tied to anyone else, it's a whole new level of freedom.

Passion

"Just follow your passion!" That's the smug advice from successful people who conveniently forget they already had money, resources, or a trad wife when they started. Passion? How the frog are you supposed to know what you're passionate *enough* about that it could be the idea for a business? How are you supposed to magically summon a passion that's strong enough to build a business around when you're drowning in bills? How do you "follow your passion" when you're numb from survival mode? When you're overwhelmed, overworked, underpaid, or so emotionally exhausted that even choosing a Netflix show feels like a major life decision. How? And, on top of all that, what if you're struggling with addiction or fighting for sobriety? Finding the energy to create some all-consuming, life-altering passion project can be difficult when you're merely trying to get through the day without losing your mind. I get it.

When I decided to start my blogging business, I didn't have a passion for blogging. But I did have a terrifying feeling bubbling under my skin that if I didn't make a financial change quickly, things could get very bad very soon. I was stressed out and tired of being poor. So, back then, I was following my passion to *not be poor anymore*. Not starving motivated me to get started. Later, as I was actually writing the blog, I discovered that I am, in fact, passionate about blogging. Obsessively so! I freakin' love it now.

Of course, some people will share their opinion that starting a business only to make money is a bad thing. Well, I'm telling you that they are either lying or in denial. If someone doesn't believe that needing money is a good reason to start a business, then they've probably never been close to homelessness or lived the reality of having zero financial support from family and no safety net. Maybe they've never stayed too long in a bad, abusive relationship because they couldn't afford to get their own place right away. Perhaps they've never felt the embarrassment of lining up at the food bank. I've experienced all of that. So, I can say with one hundred percent certainty that wanting to make money is fine. In fact, I'd argue that starting a business with profit as your number one goal is simply common sense. If you aren't focused on revenue as an entrepreneur, then consider that you might actually be building an expensive hobby, not a business.

If you have ever experienced poverty or homelessness, then you know it's a privilege to be able to launch a business *without* having to think about money. "Don't focus on the money; just focus on your passion!" sounds like a cruel joke when you're calculating how much you can stretch a bag of rice. ("I'd be able to find my passion if I weren't so burnt out from just trying to survive!" the chorus sings.)

Getting myself out of the hole was priority number one. And blogging was the vehicle to do it. In the process of building that blog, I ended up discovering my passions. Not the other way around. Your story might be different. Sure, many projects have become successful businesses because the owner was super passionate about the niche, product, or message. But that's not the only way. You can also start a business, like I did, out of sheer desperation to make money, to not starve to death. One is not more or less noble or superior than the other. You can become passionate about things later once you're fed.

Some people know what their passions are from a young age, and it doesn't change. For others, as adults, finding something to be passionate about and keeping a high level of interest in it isn't easy or obvious.

You might not know what your passion is right now, and that's okay. Passion isn't something most adults find; it's something they build. And they don't build it by sitting around waiting for inspiration to strike. No, they build it by taking action and experimenting. By figuring out what doesn't make you want to yeet your laptop out of a window. (Side note: Do the kids still say *yeet*?)

For most adults, passion isn't something you find; it's something you build. And you don't build it by sitting around waiting for inspiration to strike. No, you build it by taking action and experimenting. By figuring out what doesn't make you want to yeet your laptop out of a window. (Side note: Do the kids still say 'yeet'?).

If you weren't handed a passion in life at inception, you will need to work at figuring out what you enjoy. Try everything, read, listen, learn. Get out of your house and pay attention to your thoughts. When you feel a spark of interest, run with it!

Or it may be that you're on the other side of the passion spectrum, where you have *too many passions*. So many, in fact, that it's impossible for you to narrow them down to only one. So you are paralyzed, unable to get *anything* going because you are overwhelmed with ideas for what you *could* do for a business that you never do anything.

To you, I say, ah yes, the multi-passionate one! You have a gazillion fiery passions, all lighting you up at once. You love fashion, graphic design, photography, wellness, business strategy, vintage furniture restoration, video games, boat racing and more. Somehow, you've convinced yourself that in order to be successful, you must pick just one, marry it, and commit for life. And that's a choice too difficult to attempt. No wonder you're paralyzed.

Say it with me: "I do NOT have to choose one passion forever!" Just choose one to start with. Because right now, you're playing a dangerous game of mental pinball. Bouncing between ideas, endlessly researching, and never actually launching anything because you're scared of "choosing wrong."

So, how do you break free from analysis paralysis and actually *do* something? Begin here:

1. **Stop looking for "the one."** Your business is not your soulmate. You are not committing to it for life. You are choosing a starting point. Pick something, test it, see how it feels, and know that you can (and will) pivot later. Your first business won't be your last.

2. **Choose the easiest door to walk through.** Out of all your interests, which one is the fastest and most straightforward to monetize? Start there. Make money first. Get fancy later.

3. **Combine your passions in a way that makes sense.** Suppose you love design, writing, and business strategy. Boom! Brand consulting. Are you obsessed with wellness, cooking, and content creation? Start a wellness blog with digital recipe products. If you're into AI, entrepreneurship, and social media, then teach people how to automate their content creation. You're the common denominator here. It's your unique mix of interests that makes your business different.

4. **Take imperfect action.** Pick ONE idea and give yourself

> a week to create something tangible, whether it's a website, an offer, a sales page, a product, or whatever. And, if you hate it? Change it later. At least you're moving. Take it from me, success doesn't come from picking the "perfect" idea. It comes from taking messy, imperfect action and figuring it out as you go. So stop waiting for clarity to magically appear. Pick an idea, take action, and trust that the right path will reveal itself once you actually start walking.

Pick one thing so you can move forward. Later, you can create new offers, experiment, build a business in a totally different niche, or whatever else. But you need to get the ball rolling. It doesn't have to be your life's passion, and honestly, you will probably suck at your first business anyway. So, you may as well save your life's passion for a future business endeavor when you have gained more skills from experience. Use this first one as the testing ground where you get to learn. Trust that the passion can come later.

Once you pick that one thing, here's the good news: Making money with an online business is easier than most people think. In some ways, it's stupid how easy it is. The hard part, for me at least, is staying interested in a business long enough to give it what it needs to succeed. I have ADHD, and I'm a Gemini, which, if you aren't into sun signs, means my attention span is scattered from dirt to the stars and beyond. It's my nature to jump from project to project, picking up a new hobby and forgetting about the last one on a rapid-fire whim. Truth be told, I rarely complete anything. Case in point, even as I am writing, I am not entirely sure I will actually finish this book. If you are reading it, know that no one is more shocked than I am that it made it to print.

Yet that fleeting interest is also my superpower, so I've learned. I know I'm not the type of entrepreneur who "operates" a business. I'm not made for working on the same project forever. However, I am made for being an ideal *acquisition entrepreneur* (aka website investor). Someone who acquires a business that needs work, improves it quickly, scales it, and sells it to someone who will run it for the long haul.

That's why website investing is so great for people like me. Being a website investor allows me to work on a project for a little while, then sell it and move on to something in a completely different niche. The constant change and adrenaline are perfect for me. It could be perfect for you, too.

The next chapters of this book will give you clear steps on how to buy and sell online businesses. You'll learn to create offers, boost traffic, and increase sales. I have also included a step-by-step plan for precisely what to do to get your offer up for sale *in one day*. For now, know that, no, you don't need some grand, burning passion to start. You just need an idea, a little curiosity, and the audacity to try.

No Princes

Contrary to what fairy tales may have led us to believe, no prince is coming to save us and hand us the life of luxury we desire. No one is going to make you start your business or force you to launch your digital product. No one is going to come into your room and make you get up early or make you exercise. And, unfortunately, no one can Airdrop their discipline to you, so you finally sit down and write your book. *It's all on you, boo.*

Yes, you have big goals. Perhaps you want to finally quit that job that drains your soul, speak on stages, or move to a city that actually excites you. Maybe you dream of financial freedom, working for yourself, or building something that revolutionizes society as we know it. But if we're being honest? You probably keep shoving at least one goal onto the back burner, never letting it cook anything real.

You tell yourself, "I'll get to it one day." "One day when I have more time." "One day, when I have more followers." "One day, when everything falls perfectly into place, my branding is perfect, and I feel fully, spiritually, financially, and emotionally ready."

STOP. RIGHT. NOW. Last I checked, "one day" is not a day that exists on the calendar. It's just a delay tactic we use when we're scared, overwhelmed, or unsure of where to start. And the longer you let your dreams sit on the back burner, the colder they get.

There is no perfect time, no magical sign from the universe that says, "Hey, now is the correct moment to chase your dreams!" The only thing that makes goals happen is deciding that today is the day to stop waiting and start moving. Action is what sets the people who make things happen apart from those who wish things would happen. Tiny, consistent actions.

Heck, I spent decades saying to myself, "I'll publish a book one day." Yet, I wasn't taking any tangible steps toward making a book real, like sitting down to map out an outline. I procrastinated working on this very book. Funny. I would write sections here and there, yet as the years passed, I never completed any chapter in full. I'd ask myself if I was lazy, unproductive, or had fears about book publishing that might be blocking me from taking it seriously.

When I looked at what I did each day, it was certainly not any of those things. I write and publish tons of content daily for my blog and newsletter. Hundreds of thousands of words every month! Every day, I pursued my creator business and worked toward my various goals.

So, what was my problem when it came to my book goal? What was different? Ah, I nearly fell off my chair when it finally dawned on me why. You see, I had just finished a coaching call with a client. She was going through a creativity block, expressing that she couldn't muster up the motivation to work on her sales page. She felt like she was waiting around forever for the interest to come back; meanwhile, she felt guilty for not doing it. Have you ever felt like that? I helped her break out of her block, and as I heard what I told her coming out of my mouth, it dawned on me that it was precisely the advice I needed, too.

What I explained was just like how no prince will be riding in to save her: no one is going to magically plop a bag of motivation into her lap. She has to do the work anyway, regardless of whether she feels like it or not. It's all about doing it yourself, *for yourself,* without any cheerleaders, savior, or praise.

Ironically, yet without realizing it for far too long, I was waiting to get around to writing this book for the same reasons as my client. Because subconsciously, on some deep, murky level, I was waiting for some prince to save me. No, not in a romantic sense.

In this case, the metaphorical prince was a publishing house. Not any particular publishing house either—any *publishing house!*

It was as if I was expecting a literary agent to come across my blog articles or my newsletter and love my work so much that they would be compelled to offer me a book deal. Surely, having discovered me via my blog, they would somehow know that I'm the right person to throw a publishing deal at. *And then, once that happened, I'd see a reason to start writing the book.*

Ugh nooo. No one is going to ride in on a horse and save you. No one is going to hand you your life glow-up. You have to save yourself and ride your own damn pony. *You need to glow up yourself.* And yeah, I needed to take my own advice. So when I realized that I was waiting to be discovered and that that was really, really stupid, I finally opened my laptop and committed myself to writing this book. This time, with the intention of self-publishing it. Shoot, I've bootstrapped and self-started every other thing in my business and life. What makes this any different? It's time to saddle up for this ride, pony girl.

So, if you're waiting for someone to show up, sprinkle some magic motivation dust on your head, and make you wake up at 5 a.m., write that blog post, launch your business, or finally go to the gym...you're going to be waiting forever. Nobody is coming. Nobody is going to swoop in and force you to take action. Not a business partner, a friend, or your dog (though, honestly, dogs are good accountability buddies).

Let's have another moment of brutal honesty, shall we? You are on your own rescue mission. Your dream life is happening right now! Seriously, your dream business isn't waiting to activate until you reach 10,000 followers. Your dream love life isn't waiting to start because you haven't found your soulmate yet. Start loving yourself now. The prince is busy working on his own shit. (It's probably a podcast of his unhinged opinions that no one asked for.)

All jokes aside, the point is that no prince is riding in on a white horse to rescue you from the hard work. No one is going to miraculously discover your talent and hand you a book deal before you've written a single page or offer you a six-figure business opportunity out of thin air.

Success doesn't happen because you wait for it; it happens because you make yourself successful. Want to be a writer? Write the damn book. Want to be a business owner? Sell something. Want to go viral? Start posting content. Consistently, and often. Want to be an expert in your field? Start showing up like one before anyone asks you to. Nobody is coming to make you take action. No mentor, no agent, no investor, no mysterious benefactor. It's you. It's always been you, you gorgeous, intelligent, funny, and capable human. So stop waiting for an invitation or permission. Put on your crown and start building the kingdom—ahem—the *Queendom,* yourself.

2

Shadow Work is Necessary

Annoying Obstacles and How to Overcome Them

As you start leveling up your life, a whole lot of hairballs will come up from within you. The stairs that lead to your best self only reveal themselves when you remove the layers of old carpet. Pull that carpet up and remediate it fast.

And no, this has nothing to do with getting a bikini wax. We're talking about doing *shadow work,* and it's an essential part of any self-improvement journey.

At the beginning stage of your life Glow-Up Plan, you will encounter tough new challenges, including imposter syndrome, Internet trolls, and public scrutiny. Those unpleasantries are par for the course. Yet, when you do your shadow work first, you'll be able to face those ghouls without spiraling.

If you skip this part, old fears, limiting beliefs, and insecurities will resurface. Much like zombies, their only purpose is to eat away at your mind.

Doing the Shadow Work

What is shadow work? It's like being your own detective. Engaging in shadow work means exploring the less ideal aspects of yourself, the hidden and overlooked parts of your personality. Then, you work on healing and improving those areas for a better you. By allowing yourself this time for self-discovery, you'll help reveal your true self. I like to think of shadow work as emotional decluttering. It's taking a deep and sometimes tough look at yourself.

You might ask, "Why do I feel unworthy of success? Why do I let fear of judgment keep me from showing up? What disappointments am I holding onto? How do I react when I feel threatened? Why do I sabotage my progress the second things start working for me? How do I react when things don't go as planned? Why do I believe I'm not smart/pretty/talented enough to deserve a good life?"

It's about recognizing the burdens we carry, such as fear, shame, old wounds, past trauma, and self-sabotage. We need to recognize them so they don't keep running the show. Peeling back the layers of the unconscious mind is like peeling an onion. It uncovers hidden strengths and weaknesses that have been influencing and shaping our lives all this time. We can read all the self-help books out there, yet if we don't heal our shadows, we'll unknowingly sabotage our success.

If you don't deal with your fears, wounds, and limiting beliefs, they will:

- Show up as imposter syndrome (convince you you're a

fraud).

- Manifest as self-sabotage: so you might procrastinate, avoid chances, or quit before starting.

- Keep you playing small (because success is scary when you secretly think you don't deserve it).

Like mushrooms that won't stop popping up all over your yard, your unhealed shiitake will haunt you. It will creep in at your highest moments and whisper, "Who do you think you are?" right when you're about to do something great. So rather than letting that happen, face your shadow now, head-on. Try this exercise.

How to Do Shadow Work in Four Steps:

1. **Write down what you're afraid of people seeing in you**. What "flaws" are you terrified people will notice? What parts of yourself do you try to hide? What judgments do you fear the most? Congratulations, you've just met your shadow.

2. **Ask where that fear came from**. Who made you believe you aren't good enough? What past experiences convinced you that success isn't safe? What beliefs did you pick up as a kid that no longer serve you? Awareness is half the battle.

3. **Reframe the narrative**. The thing you're ashamed of

is potentially your superpower. The thing you're hiding? It's the key to your authenticity. The thing you think makes you unworthy? It's what will make people trust and relate to you.

4. **Let that BS go**. Rewrite the story you tell yourself. Decide what gets to be true about you from now on. Yes, work on the areas that need improvement, but don't overfocus on them because what you focus on, you create more of! Don't take on the identity of what you need to work on. Instead, attend to who you are now. Step into who you actually are, not who your past convinced you you are.

If you skip shadow work, old fears can control you. They'll pull you back into self-doubt, procrastination, and small thinking. But when you face your shadows, you become unstoppable. Before we move on to the next part (dealing with public scrutiny and handling trolls), take a moment to face your shadows. Sit with them and then let them go. Because the next phase of your life will require a version of you that is no longer ruled by the past.

For a list of 100 questions to heal your shadow, visit the bonus vault at GlowUpYourself.com/bonus

Hello Cringe

It takes a lot of guts to be the face of your brand and build a business on the Internet. The *big* kind of guts. The kind that allows you to hit "publish" on something that makes you want to throw your phone into a swamp immediately. Because let's be real, putting yourself out there, especially in the beginning, feels cringey. And if it never does? You're probably not entrepreneuring hard enough.

Starting a business is already nerve-wracking. But starting a business *publicly,* well, that's a whole different level of terror. Your first Instagram Live? Awkward. Your first blog post? Probably a mess. Your first webinar? A technical disaster waiting to happen.

However, you must embrace the cringe because that's the only way to improve. If you have goals of reaching success, prepare to climb "Cringe Mountain."

Coined by Erica Mallett, Cringe Mountain is that period of awkwardness and embarrassment when you're trying something new. She says:

> "Everyone who is now cool or good at something at some point had to climb Cringe Mountain. But you can't descend to The Land Of Cool without going over Cringe Mountain. Anyone who laughs at you for being cringe, they're looking up at you from down at the bottom. They haven't even started climbing!"
>
> - Erica Mallett @erica_mallett

Cringe Mountain is steep, but once you reach the top, you've made it. It's no longer cringe at the top, nor is it cringe on the journey back down the other side to The Land of Cool. We all face the journey up Cringe Mountain. Only those who keep going reach the top. They don't turn back, saying, "Never mind, this is too embarrassing." No one starts as an expert. The pro was once a beginner who didn't quit when they felt ridiculous.

Now, here's a question. Who, exactly, are you afraid will think you're cringe? Your friends and family? People from your hometown? Your middle school bully? Your judgy great-aunt who still thinks Facebook is the whole Internet? I can bet that none of them have tried to climb Cringe Mountain. Do you know who has? Every single successful entrepreneur you admire. No one at the top would ever shame someone for trying.

When reflecting on this idea of Cringe Mountain on her TikTok, career coach Courtney Johnson stated that when you launch your first podcast, a successful podcaster isn't going to DM you and say, "Worst thing I've ever heard." When you start posting videos on YouTube, a successful YouTuber isn't going to comment, "This sucks." If anything, they would hype you up because they remember when they started out. And that's the difference.

The people at the top aren't judging you. They're cheering for you. Yes, you will look and feel silly at first. Your production quality probably won't be that great. And your content, performance, and graphics will most likely look amateur. Well, duh! That's because you are an amateur right now! *Keep going! Embrace the cringe!* Because how else will you learn to improve if you don't keep trying? Professionals got that way with experience. The more you tackle this, the more experience you gain, and the better you become. With practice, you'll sharpen your skills and soon become a pro, too. You must overcome the worry about who is watching or what they think.

I get it. Oh, girl, I get it. Your friends and family who knew you as the before "you," the one before you became a creator and an entrepreneur, are not used to seeing you that way. They will most likely find it weird when you start posting about your workshops and products. After all, those people have only known you to post about your personal life until now. And they are comfortable with *that* version of you. Now, all of a sudden, you are a business owner, posting about your business, clients, and offers? Well, they weren't expecting that from you, and they might not get the vision right away.

So what? It's a new era for you. They can either get on board or not. Their approval is not required by you. Nor does their approval pay your bills.

But yes, as you start climbing, you'll meet some unsavory characters on the way up. Some will be in real-time (*hello, Internet trolls),* while others will be imagined *(hello, traumatic memories of a middle school bully!*) And, of course, your own inner critic (*Oh, hi there, imposter syndrome! You little biatch!*) We will cover Internet trolls and imposter syndrome in a moment. But first, we need to deal with the bullies of the past whose memories won't seem to stay in the past.

Bullies

Girl bullies are different from boy bullies. Just like ADHD in girls, the tactics girl bullies use often go unseen by adults. Instead of the physical punch a boy bully throws down to abuse someone, girl bullies employ bone-chilling, non-physical *psychological* terror on their victims.

These leave invisible mental wounds that never really heal. My middle school bully still pops up in my mind sometimes, decades later, usually whenever I'm about to do something big, like speak on stage or try something new in my business. I can feel her judging me and taunting me to fail. Does that ever happen to you?

Isn't it wild? You can be a full-grown adult—paying bills, running a business, and maybe even raising actual human children—and the second you try to do something new, a ghost from seventh grade materializes. "Oh hey, remember that time you farted in the cafeteria? Yeah, you're still that person."

The echoes of the times we were told to quiet down, fit in, and not be too much stick with us. When we got laughed at for trying and felt like an outsider, convinced that taking up space was an inconvenience to all. Then, when we're on the verge of something big like starting a business, showing up online, asking for more, or betting on ourselves...boom! The ghosts of middle school past show up with their "you-can't-sit-with-us" energy, baiting us to stay small.

Thinking about my seventh-grade bully, I realize that a punch from her bony fists would have been better than what she delivered instead. Let's journey back to the summer of 1997. "Song 2" by Blur, "Creep" by TLC, and "Sunday Morning" by No Doubt were *the* soundtracks to my summer. My style was a mix between Lisa "Left Eye" Lopes, a Spice Girl, and Gwen Stefani in her "Just a Girl" phase. One day, I'd be in baggy jeans and Doc Martens. The next day, I'd wear a baby doll dress with sparkly platform sandals. Then, I'd switch to plaid hip-huggers, a cropped tank with studded bra straps, and stick-on diamonds under my eyes. *I was a whole vibe*.

I had just turned twelve, and I had two best girlfriends my age. The three of us were inseparable that summer. We would roam around Semiahmoo Shopping Center for hours. Our favorite pastime was browsing the racks at Mariposa to create outfits inspired by Cher from *Clueless* or our favorite Spice Girl. We'd snap photos of our looks in the changing rooms but never buy anything. Sorry, Mariposa. Warm nights were spent under the stars, wading through the ocean at White Rock Beach, our bikes and clothes tossed in the sand, miles away. We were convinced that our lives would be that sweet forever. We were tiptoeing on the line between childhood and adolescence and about to become teenagers *together*. What could be better?

Then, just like that, my world imploded. My mom hit me with the kind of news that makes your stomach drop straight into the earth's core. She announced that we were *moving*. To a new town. Miles away. Away from my friends, my life, everything I knew. Absolute devastation. Even worse, the town I was being forced to move to didn't even have a mall! Can you believe the audacity? But that's not even the craziest part. Get this: you couldn't even drive there. You had to get there by BOAT. It was a freaking ISLAND with a population of 1,200 people. *Were we going into the witness protection program?! What the heck was my mom up to?!* Alright, a peaceful island town might sound like a lovely place to live (nowadays, I'd agree), but at the age of twelve, it was my worst nightmare.

My mom had given birth to my brother a year before, and she and his dad had just broken up. Now I get that she was ready for a fresh start. But at the time, I was frustrated by the abrupt lifestyle change imposed on me. She packed my brother and me into a moving truck and left life in White Rock behind. I entered seventh grade at a new little school on Pender Island, not knowing anyone. Here, I struggled to make friends and somehow managed to become the target of the resident bully. Her real name was so perfect for a bully that I wish I could use it here. But I can't. So let's just call her Bruty.

Bruty was a scary young lady with an under-shave haircut. She ruled the roost at the school and didn't like a new "city bitch" moving in on her coop. The townsfolk in this small island community were used to the status quo of simple attire. My whole Cher-Gwen-Left-Eye-Spice-Girl-inspired wardrobe was pretty out there for that place. And Bruty made it clear that my presence, sparkly platforms and all, was unwanted.

Bruty would hand out icy, hateful remarks here and there. Usually, she didn't even have to say a word, and you'd still crumble if you saw her coming. She would merely stare you down, and your insides would roll over. She didn't need to throw a punch or even threaten you with physical pain because her power was 100% psychological terror. Bruty decided I was a loser and made it her mission in life to make everyone else in school agree. She taunted me daily.

I wasn't the only one; she had a few victims on her roster. Another girl in my class suffered a UTI because she was too scared to go to the bathroom for fear of running into her. So yeah, it was bad. I was terrified to go to school. Each day, the pit in my stomach hurt more. Anxiety, insecurity, fear of scrutiny, and fear of not being good enough; it all started there, folks.

Fortunately, Bruty moved away at the end of the school year, and I never saw her again. Unfortunately, the impression she made on my psyche stuck around. It sucks, but bad-energy people like that can affect you mentally, even years after they're gone. Decades have passed, and even now, as a grown woman, I still catch myself at times feeling those same anxious terror feelings I felt at twelve years old.

Whenever I have to speak on stage, do a podcast interview, or generally put myself out there for my business, it's not uncommon for the spine-chilling essence of Bruty to pop up in my head and judge me. If you've ever experienced the misery of being bullied at a young age, you might relate. Isn't it strange that even as adults, far removed from our childhood bullies, we can still be affected by them? Yet, I like to think that being reminded of those feelings is also a reminder of how far we've come. We've lived through the Brutys of the world, and we still get up, turn on the camera, and create.

How to Expel Your Inner Bullies:

1. **Recognize that the voice isn't yours.** That doubtful, critical voice in your head? It's not you. It's an old tape, replaying words that were never true to begin with. The next time it creeps in, pause and ask, "Whose voice is this?" Because it sure as hell isn't coming from future you.

2. **Rewrite the script**. Replace every "What if I fail?" with "What if I succeed?" Replace every "I'm not good enough" with "I'm figuring it out, and that's enough."

3. **Actively reject the mean girl BS**. Your middle school bully isn't here. They don't get a vote. The only person who decides what happens next is you. So act accordingly. This time around, YOU are the one telling them that they can't sit with YOU (in your mind, that is).

4. **Prove yourself to...yourself**.Forget trying to prove people wrong. Prove yourself RIGHT. Take action, take up space, and let your success be the loudest mic drop in history.

5. **Move like you've already won**.Because you have. You made it through the hard stuff.

Fact: Those schoolyard bullies from your past don't get to graduate with you. They flunked out. You're the principal now, and it's time for you to expel them from your mind. You have outgrown them and outlived their relevance. The version of you that was once shy, unsure, and self-conscious? She put in her time and survived. Now, it's your turn to thrive. Welcome to your glow-up era. No bullies allowed.

Imposter Syndrome

Imposter syndrome is the obnoxious little voice in your head whispering total bull to you like, "You're not qualified to do this," and "Sooner or later, they're gonna figure out you have no idea what you're doing and expose you as a fraud." It's the anxiety-loving, sneaky little brat that lives rent-free in your brain that is always jeering at you, always summoning up feelings of self-inadequacy. Even though you are *perfectly adequate, thank you very much.*

My understanding of this concept expanded when I read Jen Sincero's *You Are A Badass* book series. Jen refers to imposter syndrome as the "Little Prince" who lives inside us. She describes this prince as the tiny, panicky, self-doubting voice inside you that freaks out whenever you try to step outside your comfort zone. The Little Prince is that whiny, overprotective friend who means well but also insists you stay exactly where you are, forever, because change is scary and success is unknown territory. He whispers things like:

- You don't know what you're doing! You're going to embarrass yourself.

- What if people find out you're not an expert?

- You should definitely wait until you have a master's degree, 10 years of experience, and a handwritten letter of approval from the Galactic Federation before you even think about launching this thing.

According to Jen, you don't get rid of the Little Prince. Nope, he's here for the ride, whether you like it or not. The *trick,* however, is to recognize it for what it actually is: your fear, your self-doubt, your subconscious clinging to "safety." Then, proceed to ignore him like a LinkedIn connection request from a guy who claims to want to network but is definitely going to pitch you his crypto scheme.

The most annoying part? Imposter syndrome doesn't go away just because you get more successful. Actually, the higher you climb, the louder imposter syndrome gets. If you think you're the only one who has ever felt like you're not good enough, oh honey, welcome to the club.

- When nominated to the Rock & Roll Hall of Fame, Dolly Parton initially turned it down. She acknowledged experiencing imposter syndrome and felt she hadn't earned it. Yes. THAT Dolly Parton felt like a fraud.

- Sheryl Sandberg, the former COO of Meta, has said she often felt unqualified for her job. This was while she was successfully running one of the biggest companies in the world.

- Simone Biles has spoken about her struggle with imposter syndrome. She often feels unworthy of her successes. This is despite collecting eleven Olympic medals and thirty World Championship medals, the most of any gymnast in history.

Do you see a theme here? Imposter syndrome doesn't mean you're not good enough. It means you're human. It means you're pushing past your comfort zone, doing something bigger than yourself, and actually giving a hoot.

I'm no stranger to imposter syndrome, let me tell you. When I was a teenager, I heard that a TV show was holding nationwide auditions to form the next big pop star girl group. To my delight, they were making a stop at a mall in Victoria that weekend. Obviously, I HAD to go. I managed to get the day off from my very glamorous dishwashing job and took the ferry to Vancouver Island. I bussed into Victoria, dashed into the mall, and got in line to sign up. I had zero doubt that this was going to be my big break. I was ready to make history.

But when I finally reached the sign-up table, it all came crashing down. The woman behind the desk looked at my form and said, "You need a parent's signature to audition. You're a minor."

Oh no! I was here on a solo pop star mission, and my mom was nowhere near Victoria. She was back on my home island, hours away. I had come all this way for nothing. Defeated, I walked away, feeling my dreams of superstardom evaporate into the food court air. I was about to exit the mall and slump back onto the bus when a woman approached me. "I'll be your mom and sign for you," she offered. A saint of a woman, my guardian angel in yoga pants. I said yes, obviously, and just like that, I was back in the game.

I was directed to another line after "my mom" signed for me. At the end of this line, there was a stage in the middle of the mall where I would have to sing a cappella in front of an entire crowd of strangers. At first, I was fine. I had this. I was born for this. I was already imagining my dramatic, post-audition interview where I would humbly tell the producers, "I've always known I was meant for stardom." Then, the girl in front of me started talking.

She casually mentioned that she was a professionally trained vocalist. She had done competitions, showcases, private lessons, and recitals. She used words like resonance, cadence, and *projection*. She had a vocal coach. I did not have a vocal coach. I had a hairbrush microphone and a dream. Well, just like that, imposter syndrome appeared, ready to audition to take the role of my confidence.

Suddenly, my assurance collapsed like an overstuffed taco. My mind whirled. *I've never trained for this. I've never auditioned for anything. I've never even sung in front of a crowd. I am about to embarrass myself in front of an entire shopping mall.* The line kept moving. Every step forward felt like I was walking toward a slow, inevitable public humiliation. My armpits got hot. My stomach turned. *Why is it so hot in here?*

The professionally trained singer in front of me was now doing vocal exercises. What even were vocal exercises? I had never done one in my life. One person before it was her turn. Then I was next, the point of no return. And I panicked. I tore off my contestant number, stepped out of line, and walked straight back into the crowd. I told myself it was fine; I just did not feel like auditioning today. Doo-da-doo.

I watched from the audience as the girl who had just sent me into a full-blown crisis of confidence walked onto the stage. She took a breath and opened her mouth..., and I realized how ridiculous I had been. Because, friends, she could not sing. Like, seriously, girlfriend could not sing. I am talking donkey braying with a car alarm level of bad. She gave an entire symphony of off-key notes, like a karaoke performance gone horribly, hilariously off the rails.

At that moment, I knew I had let a whole lot of talk and my fears ruin my shot at trying. She had been all confidence, no delivery. And I had been all doubt, no courage. Maybe I would have been just as bad or far worse, but I'll never know. She was the only one brave enough to give it a try.

The funny thing about imposter syndrome is that it only shows up when you are about to do something that actually matters. It's never there when you're doing something safe and small. It arrives right when you are about to take a leap. At that moment, you have two choices. You can let it convince you that you are not ready, that you do not belong, that everyone else knows something you don't. Or you can realize that everyone is also just figuring it out as they go.

That girl had no business shaking my confidence the way she did. And yet, I let her. The show came out a few months later. I watched as the pop group I was too scared to audition for formed on my TV screen. I tuned in weekly to watch as they recorded their album, and made their first music video. *Darn. I would have loved doing those things.*

Yet I've had more run-ins with imposter syndrome since my popstar audition-avoiding days, especially as a business owner. When I booked an author known for her confident, cool-girl personality as a guest on my podcast, I was on top of the world. She was going to be on my show to discuss her new book. She sent me a prerelease copy, and I dove into it before our interview. I was pumped. Until I wasn't.

As the recording day crept closer, my brain went into full-blown imposter mode. *This woman is so cool! Too cool! She's going to regret saying yes to doing this interview the second she meets me. She's going to realize I'm not cool. I'm not a professional. I will stumble over my words and sound like a total amateur.*

Even though it disguised itself as nervousness, perfectionism, and having my best interests at heart (Oh, I should probably reschedule because I want to be fully prepared), in reality, it was 100% sneaky imposter syndrome debauchery at its finest. The night before our recording, my nerves tried to convince me to reschedule and skip it entirely. Oh no, I'm suddenly coming down with an extremely convenient case of 'I'M NOT WORTHY'-itis.

That was until I read the final chapters of her book, when I read a story that slapped me out of my nonsense. She shared her experience at a wellness retreat. She was having a tough time, yet felt hopeful about having met a possible new friend. They had planned to go to dinner together. Then, when she went to pick her up, there was a note on the door. The woman wrote that she had decided not to meet up. Specifically, she wrote that she feared the author would discover she wasn't cool enough to hang out with. So she bailed.

The woman left the retreat the next day, and the author never got to tell her she was wrong. Or that she had been looking forward to that dinner. That she wanted to connect. That the woman's self-doubt had cost them both something that could have been really great.

That's when I realized, Oh. My. God. Here I was thinking about canceling on her, too. I was just like that girl at the wellness retreat. My imposter syndrome made me feel too intimidated by the author, too. Having made this connection, there was no way I was going to do that to her now. There was no way I was going to do that to myself.

So I snapped out of it, stuck to the plan, and showed up. Guess what? The interview went incredibly well. We had a fantastic conversation; the author was warm, engaging, and hilarious. Shockingly, She didn't regret coming on my show. If I had let imposter syndrome win, I would have missed that talk, that experience, and that growth moment.

Moral of the story: Stop assuming people are "too cool" for you. Or that you don't deserve to be where you are. Stop canceling on yourself before you even start. You belong in the room. You belong at the table. You belong in the conversation. Most importantly, imposter syndrome isn't a warning that you're underqualified. It's a sign that you're leveling the hell up.

Newbie? You'll feel it. Expert? You'll feel it. The fact remains that you only fail when you take yourself out of the game. So whatever it is you are hesitating about, whatever you are overthinking or are convinced you are "not ready" for yet, why not step up and do it anyway? Honestly, there is a good chance that the person you are so intimidated by doesn't know what they are doing either. Everyone experiences imposter syndrome at some point. But you have to push through it and do your work anyway. And that's precisely what you're going to do, too. It's time to call out imposter syndrome for the lying little player-hater it is and give you vital strategies to shut it down. So you can move forward with confidence. The world doesn't need another brilliant woman holding herself back. It needs you, doing the thing unapologetically. So how do we put this into action so you can break free from "one day I'll do it" reruns and stop letting imposter syndrome run the show?

Here's a step-by-step process for dealing with your inner player hater, imposter syndrome:

Step 1. Accept that imposter syndrome is a rite of passage. You might feel it when you launch a new offer or when you appear on a podcast. It will suddenly feel like you don't belong or you don't have the expertise to be the spokesperson for your brand. Imposter syndrome doesn't mean you don't deserve to be there; it just means you're venturing out of your comfort zone and are in new territory. It means you care enough about what you're doing to want to not suck at it.

Step 2. Acknowledge it's happening and move on. Recognize imposter syndrome for what it is, a knee-jerk fear response, *heavy on the jerk.* When imposter syndrome shows up, acknowledge its arrival: Oh, hey buddy, I see you're here again, reminding me of all the ways I could fail. Adorable. Thanks for looking out.

Shame it: Wow, what a predictable little fear-mongering ding-dong you are. Move on: Sorry, too busy being awesome to entertain this nonsense today. BLOCKED. When you recognize it and call it out, it makes it way less powerful. The goal is not about never experiencing imposter syndrome. The goal is not to let it take the wheel.

Step 3. Do the thing anyway. The only way to prove your player-hater wrong is to take action, get results, and show that it's full of crap. The reality is that Imposter Syndrome doesn't go away just because you hit six figures. It doesn't magically disappear when you get a book deal, land a client, or become the expert people look up to. It just gets quieter the more you prove to yourself that you're capable. So, let it whine in the background while you level up.

Step 4. Reframe the fear. That pit in your stomach when you try something new? That's not proof that you suck. That's proof that you care. Reframe the fear as excitement: Instead of "What if I fail?" think, "What if this actually works?" Instead of "Who am I to do this?" ask yourself, "Who am I not to do this?" Instead of "What if people judge me?" ask, "What if they love it? What if it changes someone's life?"

I also like keeping a "Proof" folder handy whenever imposter syndrome creeps in. You need cold, hard receipts that you are, in fact, a baddie.

Keep a Proof folder where you save:

- Nice things people have said about your work.
- Success stories and wins (no matter how small)

- Results you have brought to your clients.
- Moments when you did something scary and survived.

When self-doubt hits, open the folder and remind yourself that you're not just "faking it." You've already done great things, and you're just getting started.

Also, remember that nobody knows WTF they're doing. Do you think all those super-successful, ultra-confident entrepreneurs have some secret manual to success? Nope. They're winging it. Everyone is winging it!. No one has it all figured out; they're just throwing spaghetti at the wall until something sticks. Sure, pros may have figured out more than amateurs, but they will never have it all figured out. Because algorithms, trends, and public interest constantly change. Even people at the top, must be willing to learn new things and adapt to stay relevant.

When you realize this, you'll feel oh-so free. Success isn't about knowing everything. It's about knowing enough to start and being willing to figure the rest out as you go.

If you're thinking, "Okay, Chelsea, but I still feel like an imposter..." GOOD. Your imposter syndrome only has game if it can get to you, but you're a tough chick now! You aren't going to fall for its weak attempts to sabotage you anymore.

The player-hater is officially under a restraining order. Now, put your blinders on and do the work.

Trolls

Congratulations! You're setting out to launch a business on the Internet, which means you're doing something bold, visible, and worth talking about. And the reward for that? A front-row seat to the peanut gallery of unsolicited opinions, criticism, and people who have somehow made it their life's mission to make sure you feel bad about yourself. Welcome to the club. *This part sucks!* The truth is, though, you can use criticism and troll nonsense to your advantage.

Accept that the moment you step outside of acceptable, play-it-safe, don't-make-waves territory, someone is going to have a problem with you. Maybe it's a troll in your comments, a client who didn't book but still wants to tell you what you should be doing, or even your own family side-eyeing your ambitions like you just announced you're quitting everything to become a mermaid influencer. (It sounds kind of fun doesn't it?) The faster you get comfortable with not being liked by everyone, the faster you will win.

Say it with me: "Not everyone is going to like me, and that's okay." This is a fact of life. Not a single successful person on this planet hasn't had haters. Taylor Swift has haters. Pamela Anderson has haters. If literal goddesses of talent, success, and generosity have people talking shit about them, what makes you think you'll be the exception?

Seriously, even people who simply post cute videos of puppies having fun have haters! Let that sink in. Trying to make everyone like you is the fastest way to water yourself down into a bland, boring, people-pleasing glump. And no one follows, respects, or buys from a glump.

So, stop trying to win over people who won't ever buy from you anyway. That's like pitching a steakhouse to a group of vegans. They're not your people.

Helpful criticism comes from people who want to see you improve and succeed. They offer honest, constructive feedback and are invested in your success. These people? Keep them. On the other hand, baseless, snarky, troll criticism comes from people projecting their insecurities, jealousy, or unresolved emotional baggage onto you. Not your baggage to carry.

Before you spiral over a mean comment, ask yourself:

- Is this feedback from someone whom I respect?
- Is there actually something constructive here?
- Or is this just someone spewing negativity because they hate themselves?

If it's not constructive, send it straight into the mental trash bin. You've got bigger things to do than cater to people who can only marinate in loser energy. Most troll comments do not even deserve a response from you. You don't have to attend every argument you're invited to. Let that one sink in.

Let's also consider that criticism says more about *them* than you. Someone who trolls tends to spew negativity because they are unhappy with their own life, appearance, or lack of success and wish to bring others down to their level. Their mean behavior is a reflection of how they feel about themselves. It has nothing to do with you. Successful, happy, confident, hot people don't waste time trying to disrespect others. Remind yourself you don't have any haters, just a few observers who could stand to love themselves more.

Mantra: *"I've never been put down by someone hotter than me."*

Finally, you're probably doing something right if you're being talked about. The worst thing that can happen to your business isn't criticism. It's being ignored. If people have opinions about you, you're making an impact. You're visible. You're doing something worth talking about. And that is powerful.

Think of the most successful entrepreneurs, thought leaders, and creatives. Do they have people who love them? Yes. Do they have people who hate them? Also yes. Do they let that stop them? Absolutely not.

Know that your people will find and love you for who you are. For every person who doesn't like you, there are 10 more who will love you. The trick is not to waste time convincing the wrong people when you could be focusing on the right ones. Your job is not to be liked by everyone. Your job is to show up fully as yourself, unapologetically, and let the right people discover you.

Do you want to stay small and safe, or do you want to build something great and risk not being everyone's cup of matcha? Remember that no one who's doing better than you is talking sh*t about you. People only criticize from the cheap seats. So let the trolls troll. Let the critics critique. Honestly, it's just more engagement for your posts, and that's a slay.

Prosperous Omen

After I graduated from university during The Great Recession, I was frustrated for a long time. By 2010, a full two years into the '08 recession, I'd almost lost all hope of ever putting my degree to use. I had applied to countless jobs in Vancouver and was interviewed and shortlisted for many, but I still hadn't landed a "real" job. I had my restaurant waitressing gig, but it was just not fulfilling, ya know?

Around this time, I set up a website to dropship women's clothing. Dropshipping is when you list items for sale that you don't actually, physically have. When someone buys it off your website you buy the item for cheap from a manufacturer (typically in China) who ships the item directly to your customer. You don't have to deal with shipping headaches or manage any inventory, as the manufacturer handles such logistics, and you keep all the profit. The website made a few sales here and there, not much, but enough to give me some spending money. Heck, dropshipping was something I could do from anywhere, so I thought, why not travel somewhere for a bit? Maybe it was my love of Latin music and burritos. Or perhaps I didn't want to endure another Canadian winter. Regardless, I was in my mid-twenties; what better place to visit than the City of Angels?

I booked a flight and a hostel, and planned to stay in Hollywood for a few months. Although I knew I couldn't afford to stay at a hostel for long. So I put an ad on Craigslist, looking for a place where I could be a short-term roommate. While waiting to board the plane, I received a reply. It was a woman named Seo-Yeon, who said she had a spare room. Would I like to meet her to see if it's a good fit?

I met Seo-Yeon the next day at The Grove. She was a beautiful Korean woman in her forties. Sunny, vibrant, and upbeat. She had a husband named Jun and two daughters, each under six. She explained that in her culture, it is normal for a whole family to sleep in the same room, and so they did. So that left them with a spare room in their two-bedroom condo.

Seo-Yeon and Jun ran a small women's clothing store on Melrose Avenue and had big plans to expand the brand. She liked that I ran my own little women's clothing store online and that I had taken marketing classes at university. We hit it off. I moved out of my hostel and in with them the next day. That night, I joined the whole family as they gathered around the TV to watch a K-pop talent show.

While living with the lovely Korean family, I would tag along on Seo-Yeon's trips downtown to the fashion district, where she'd buy clothing for her shop. We'd visit different suppliers, find the coolest items, and pack them into her minivan. Then, we'd drive back to her store to fill the racks. She'd give me business advice on these trips, and I'd pick her brain about how she got started. How did she open a real-life retail location? It blew my mind when she revealed, "You only need $10,000 to open a store." I listened intently as we drove through Hollywood. "Just get a business license, lock in a good lease, and start small with a small product line. Buy items low, and price them high enough that you have enough profit to reinvest back into the business." I'd later learn that Seo-Yeon's name means "prosperous omen" in Korean, so she knows what she's talking about.

While in Hollywood for those few months, I reconnected with a girl named Kylie, whom I'd met back home in Vancouver. She had moved to Hollywood the year before to pursue acting and was thriving in her element there. She had a beautiful apartment in a character building right in Hollywood. Kylie was quick-witted, inquisitive, and beautifully captivating. She took me under her wing and brought me along to events, restaurants, house parties, and premieres.

One night, we got so wasted at a DJ pop-up that we snuck into the VIP area, and when the Chad bros weren't looking, I hid a giant vodka bottle up my dress. Kylie and I made a beeline for the exit and ran down the street laughing like the insane clown posse we absolutely were, escaping before any of the VICs (Very Important Chads) noticed their booze had vanished.

When Kylie and I both went through breakups the same week, we headed to the nearest tattoo shop. There, she and I got swear words inked on the inside of our lower lips. That will show those jerks! LOL, I love girlhood so much. When it was time for me to return to Canada, Kylie and I promised to stay to see each other again, but I didn't know when that would be. Boarding the flight to Vancouver, I felt sad to be leaving her and sunny California behind. I watched the coastline fade into the clouds and wondered, what happens now?

Exorcism

We've been on a roll here evicting imposter syndrome, kicking out Internet trolls, and ghostbusting the middle school bullies who tried to haunt your subconscious. So, really, what better time to tell you about the time a guy tried to exorcise a demon out of me?! Yeah. That happened.

Let me preface this by saying, with 1000% certainty, that at no point in my life have I ever been possessed by a demon or been involved in anything occult. I'm all about good vibes, positivity, light, and love regarding the human and spiritual experience. And although I do believe that different levels of consciousness can exist, I don't think that demons are a real thing. Low-vibration entities exist, maybe. But nothing that can actually hurt you. (Your frequency is way too high for that; low-vibe entities can't even see you!)

This guy, let's call him Dave, who happened to be my boyfriend at the time, thought differently. His paranoia was on another level. And what unfolded next? Well, buckle up.

It all started innocently enough. Dave and I were having a completely normal chat about aliens and psychic abilities. You know, as one does. That's when I mentioned a time I almost got scammed by a psychic on Sunset Blvd. He listened intently as I explained how I was walking along when a woman handed me her business card and said in a serious tone, "Someone has put a demon inside you. I can remove it, but you'll need to book a series of readings with me." Classic Hollywood hustle. A great sales pitch, honestly.

The real kicker? The next day, I saw her pulling the exact same move on another random person. What are the odds?! Two demon-infected people, back to back? In the same exact location? I thought this scam was hilarious and assumed Dave would, too. I was wrong.

Instead of laughing, he became dead serious. His eyes grew wide, and his body tensed. He picked up his phone and started clicking.

"What are you doing?" I asked.

"I'm Googling something." A moment later, he proceeded to tell me that he needed to perform an exorcism on me. Right there. In our apartment. Immediately.

Before I could even protest, he started reciting some kind of demon-banishing spell and expected me to repeat it after him. I thought he was joking. He was not. That day, I learned Dave was not just a little stitious but superstitious. (Shout out to Michael Scott fans.)

I should also add that at the time, he had recently started smoking weed, so paranoia had entered the chat.

He was deadpan, determined. Now, at this point, I had two options, play along and pretend to cough up a demon to see how far it would go or refuse and watch him spiral further into his paranoid Google search hole.

I chose option two because, frankly, I was not about to let a psychic scam and this dude's DIY exorcism make me question my reality. I reassured him repeatedly that there was no demon, no possession, no dark entity lurking within me. Just my usual, occasionally PMS-y, fully human self. It took 48 hours before he finally let it go (probably when the ganja wore off and embarrassment set in). Yet, for those two days, he was side-eyeing me HARD as if I might start levitating at any moment.

Anyway, you might think that this little séance was the reason we inevitably broke up. But no, the real reason was far less supernatural and way more personal. You see, I realized one day that his perception of me was totally, ridiculously skewed. I had referred to myself as a woman in passing conversation by saying simply, "Yeah, it's so fun being a woman!" and he looked at me with a puzzled look on his face. The energy in the room changed. It was as if I had just let him in on the secret that I was actually a lizard.

"A what?" he replied flatly.

"A woman," I reiterated. He remained looking puzzled. "You do know I'm a woman, right?" I chuckled, thinking he'd laugh, too, because he hadn't heard me correctly the first time. Then we'd tease about how I'm so masculine, and I'd have another perfect opportunity to make a joke about my chin hair.

But he didn't laugh. He scrunched up his face and squealed, "No, *you're a girl!*"

"What are you talking about? I'm not a girl. I'm very obviously a grown woman."

He still looked confused.

"Wait... You don't consider me to be a grown woman?"

"No, a woman is like...my mom's friends."

When I tell you, I was *dumbfounded*. SIR, WHAT ARE WE EVEN DOING HERE?!

He stared blankly at me, apparently not seeing anything wrong with his lukewarm take. It was as if this was the first time he'd ever considered that the person he'd been in an exclusive relationship with (including leasing a condo together *for a year*) might be a grown adult woman.

Dave revealed, albeit unintentionally, that we had very different perceptions of our relationship. He didn't consider me to be a woman—maybe in the literal, biological sense—but not in the grown-up life-partner sense. It wasn't just a minor disconnect. This was a fundamental problem that wasn't going to change. He saw me as a girl, someone casual to hang out with until whenever. He saw no problem with chipping away at my twenties via cohabitation.

Meanwhile, I was an adult woman looking to do life stuff and build a future with another actual grown-up. It hit me that if I was going to spend my time, attention, love, and emotional labor with someone, it should be with someone who thought of me as an equal partner. And once I saw the situation for what it was, there was no unseeing it. Every day I stayed in that relationship would be another day lost, valuable time that I could be spending working on myself and building the life I actually wanted if I were single. It was time that I could use being open to meeting someone who shared my partnership-oriented views on relationships.

There is no going back once you come to such a realization. It doesn't matter how much fun someone is, how many things in common you have, or how many demons they are willing to exorcise out of you. The relationship is over.

So I made the call. It was my time to go. No hard feelings, no regrets. It is just the undeniable truth that when you realize what you truly want, you stop settling for anything less.

Side note: I learned later in life that the "there's a demon in you" scam is one of the most common tactics fake psychics use to try to trick people into buying readings from them. And nowadays, they don't just do it on the streets IRL; they do it in your DMs. So be aware of that one. A legit, gifted psychic or shaman would never try to run such a hustle on you.

Now, I do think there is something to this idea that you can exorcise unwanted energy out of yourself. Not demons per se, but rather the bad habits, past trauma, and negative beliefs that aren't serving you. As you step into a new, glowing version of yourself, you also need to let go of what's been holding you back in order to move forward into your new, positive reality.

Your current reality may be on repeat, looping the same way a bad song gets stuck in your head. You wake up, think the same thoughts, make the same choices, and get the same results. Maybe those choices haven't been the healthiest.

First, let's consider why you might be stuck in this loop. We know that our bodies and brains cling to what's familiar, good or bad. So if what's familiar is self-doubt, struggle, loneliness, or being broke, your brain will start to assume that's your normal and come to expect and even *hope for more of it*. The audacity!

For example, if, until this point, you've hesitated to put yourself out there or be seen, it might be that your mind has convinced you that visibility is a risk. Or maybe you've struggled with money for so long that your subconscious has come to expect financial stress and even tries to convince you that staying broke and struggling is normal.

Maybe your subconscious associates success with exhaustion, rejection, or burnout. Have you ever thought that burnout is necessary to succeed? Or reasoned that you're not getting ahead fast enough because you're not working hard enough?

If so, it's time to break this loop and exorcise *that* energy out of you so you can shift into the upgraded version of your best self, the one living in your best reality. Quantum identity strategist Kamari calls this a "reality override;" it's when you give your subconscious a new update, similar to overriding an old, outdated computer program.

"You don't shift by waiting. You shift by forcing a quantum-level nervous system break. Stand up and close your eyes. Imagine the version of you who stays stuck. Say out loud, "I release you, and you are no longer in control." This physically draws your body into a new state. Breathe deeply, and hold for seven seconds. Do this five times, and you will feel a nervous break in the loop. Say this three times with full certainty. "I am no longer the version who struggles. I have already shifted. My new reality is here." What happens now is your nervous system is going to glitch. You may feel lightheaded, emotional, or even laugh. That is proof that you broke the loop. This is shaking up your nervous system."

- Kamari @Quixotos.Alchemos

Kamari also recommends, after doing this, that you pay attention to what starts showing up over the next 72 hours. It may be an unexpected payment, a compliment, an act of kindness, or an opportunity. *Anything* positive. Notice and acknowledge it by declaring something like, "That's proof I'm existing in my new reality. That's my proof that my old timeline no longer exists." Now, *that's* the kind of exorcism I can get down with.

Wanted Over Worthy

If you've been spiralling in self-doubt, wondering if you're worthy of starting a business, sharing your voice, creating art, writing a book, launching a podcast, selling your work, or just taking up space in the world, I need you to stop. Right now. Because you're asking the wrong question! It's not about whether you're worthy. It's about the fact that you are *wanted*.

What I mean by this is that someone out there *wants* to hear your advice. Someone is looking for the *exact thing* you create. Someone is out there, struggling, waiting for someone like YOU to help, teach, inspire, and entertain them. And while you're sitting around wondering if you deserve to take up space, that person is still waiting. It doesn't matter if you don't have 100,000 followers yet. Do it for your one follower.

Seriously, what if you were to switch your focus from worrying about whether or not your work is worthy to *knowing* that your work is wanted? Isn't that so much more invigorating? When you believe your work is wanted, you will be less likely to self-sabotage, procrastinate, or create obstacles for yourself.

I asked celebrity coach Whitney Uland to weigh in on this. She says:

> "There's a big difference between believing you're worthy and believing you're wanted. If you don't believe people actually want your work, you'll unconsciously put up walls. That blocks you from tapping into what I call 'celebrity energy'—that magnetic vibe that draws people in. It's the energy of knowing you're desired. That people want to hear your music, binge your content, follow you, or buy your course or product. It's not just about knowing you're talented; it's about believing your work is craved. Until you subconsciously believe that, those energetic blocks will keep people at a distance."
>
> – Whitney Uland @whitneyuland

The most successful people in the world aren't the ones who are "most worthy of success." They are the ones who showed up, played it big, and let the right people find them.

"But Chels, I'm good just playing it small. I don't need to put myself out there too much!" Well, I'd suggest that playing small is the fastest way to stay broke, bored, and invisible. You don't avoid criticism by shrinking yourself. You only avoid opportunity, success, and every other It-Girl thing you're meant to do in this life.

Because here's what's actually happening when you downplay your ambitions. You let hypothetical opinions make actual decisions for you. You're handing over the keys to your life and postponing your life glow-up even longer. You're rejecting *yourself* before anyone else even gets a chance to. Successful people? They get criticized all the time. And they keep going anyway. You can either be liked by everyone and achieve nothing or be polarizing, messy, and entirely yourself and attract the people who will ride for you no matter what. The choice is yours. But I highly recommend option two.

When the pandemic struck in 2020, many 9-to-5 workers faced challenges. I saw them struggling as they lost their jobs. Without side hustles or online income, they had little to fall back on. By the time lockdowns occurred, I had been running my online business for years. I was already working remotely and was self-employed in the creator economy. I had just experienced my most profitable year, nearly seven figures, all from my blog and blog-flipping efforts. Since I had a digital business and was comfortable working from home, the pandemic didn't hit me as hard as it did many others.

The new normal of staying home for weeks on end that everyone talked about had been my normal for several years. It was so normal and so comfortable that I thought, More people should know about the creator economy. I should tell them. So, I got the idea to host a virtual summit to teach what I knew about building and flipping digital businesses. It was my first time hosting a virtual summit, and I was excited to debut it with a bang.

As I set out to plan the event, I made sure to tick every box to make the event valuable and memorable for all the attendees. It was going to be quite a production, consisting of five days of over five hours of streaming, with live and prerecorded sessions. There would be thirty-five speakers, networking parties, giveaways, bingo, a virtual DJ, and more. Everything was falling into place seamlessly. Four thousand people signed up to attend!

However, leading up to the big day, I started questioning my ability to host it. The summit was a pretty big undertaking, and a lot of people were expecting me to do a good job. As a first-time summit host, I questioned, Am I worthy of hosting this event? Am I worthy of being the one to give out this information? There's probably someone who has been earning in the creator economy for far longer than I have. Maybe they should be the host? They're probably more worthy of this size stage than I am.

Thankfully, I shook the "am I worthy" crap off before it started to stink. I reminded myself that my lived experience in the creator economy was valuable enough. And that the message I was there to teach was what mattered most. The message was *wanted*. The people who had signed up wanted to learn what I was there to give them. It didn't matter how worthy or unworthy I felt about being the facilitator. Once I shifted my focus to the fact that the information was wanted and needed rather than whether I was worthy of being the one to provide it, hosting the event became a breeze. The summit ended up being a huge success.

By holding back and worrying if you're not worthy, you're gatekeeping your greatness. Stop deciding for other people whether they need what you have to offer. The right ones do. They want it. Your creative work is wanted. Your ideas, hot takes, and innovations are wanted. And the longer you hesitate, the longer the people who want it will have to go without it. So maybe stop being selfish and just start sharing it, mmkay?

3

You Deserve to Be Rich

I am passionate about helping women become independently wealthy. Financial independence is a *necessity*. And it is *the* critical element of your life glow-up. Women who make their own money make their own rules, simple as that. They can leave toxic jobs, bad relationships, and any situation that doesn't serve them because they can afford to. And if that isn't the ultimate glow-up, I don't know what is.

Take a moment to check in with yourself. How do you feel about money, really? Light and flowy, like cash is endlessly abundant? Or are you on the other side, thinking that anyone who owns a house must have done something dirty to be able to afford it? Deep down, do you secretly believe that the wealthy are greedy, corrupt, or just lucky?

Do you think you don't *deserve* to be rich? If you grew up believing money is a limited resource, feel like talking about money is rude, taboo, or think it's about rich people rules, congratulations, you've been programmed with a Poopy Money Mindset. (Not an official condition in any journal of medicine, apparently.) If you suffer from PMM, this means that, without even meaning to, you're repelling money. Bummer. But don't worry, that's exactly what we're going to unlearn.

Think about it. How are you going to glow up yourself and start attracting millions of dollars if every inch of you is repelling money? Money gives you options, freedom, and the ability to help yourself, your family, your community, and the causes that matter to you. You deserve that. We all do.

Many of us have been subject to a lifetime of programming that has taught us that if we come into money, we will commit some debaucherous acts with it: "Money is the root of all evil." Or that if we have some money, it is a limited resource and won't come back if we spend it: "Money doesn't grow on trees." Or how about the lesson that if we receive a cash windfall, we'll lose it all because we won't know how to manage it: "Most lottery winners go broke in a year." Sound familiar?

Truth be told, I had a terrible money mindset growing up, and it lasted until I snapped out of it in my thirties. Until then, throughout my childhood and young adult life, I believed that the cards someone is dealt at birth are the cards they have to play for life. So, if you didn't come from a rich family, you had no chance of becoming well-off. If you were born into a low-income family, that was just your brand, sorry brokie.

Combine this with the belief that rich people are just lucky or did something bad to get their money, and you have a recipe for trouble! The thing is, I didn't wake up one day and decide that rich people were evil. Or even consciously realize I felt that way. That belief was absorbed, bit by bit, over years of overhearing the adults around me casually villainize wealth.

It was in the offhand comments about the well-off neighbors or nicely dressed people in a store. “Must be nice…” “I wonder what shady thing they did to afford that.” “They’re so out of touch with real life.” It was the side-eye when a guy in a nice convertible drove by: “Mid-life crisis.” It was the resentment disguised as morality. And somewhere along the way, my young brain made a connection: Having money = bad person. Struggling = normal. Which, as I later realized, is a complete load of crap.

By the time I was graduating high school, my destructive views about money had already taken root. I was amazed to hear my classmates talk about their college plans. Many had college funds all ready for them. They could pick any university they wanted, no questions asked. Tuition? Covered. Housing? Handled. That was not my reality. If I wanted to go to school, I had to figure it out.

Fortunately, my mom encouraged me to apply for scholarships. I wrote my heart out, applying for every one I could find. I was grateful to win a few based on financial need and even some based on creative merit. They partially covered tuition—great! But I still had the rest to worry about, rent, groceries, textbooks, and, well, everything else.

So I did what I had to do. I waited tables. And let me tell you, nothing warps your perception of money faster than serving $300 bottles of wine to customers while mentally calculating how many hours of tips it would take for you to afford your bag of potatoes this month. I started to feel broken because I was always behind, playing catchup, always at a disadvantage.

It seemed as though I would never reach the level of comfort those customers had. Worst of all, deep down, I still thought rich people were devious. And if I really believed that, then what the hell was I working so hard for? To become one of "them"? Subconsciously, I was pushing money away, rejecting opportunities, and staying small. Because somewhere in my head, I had linked wealth with being selfish, greedy, or disconnected from reality.

One day, it hit me. The problem wasn't that rich people were bad. The problem was that I had been taught that staying broke was noble. Who does that actually serve? Being broke didn't make me a better person. It didn't allow me to help anyone else or make life easier, more meaningful, or more virtuous.

With this breakthrough, I had to reprogram my brain to see money as a tool, not a moral test. Just like being broke doesn't make you a good person, having money doesn't make you a bad person. Money is neutral. It's not good or bad. How you use it determines everything. Wealth amplifies who you already are. If you're kind and generous when you're broke, you'll be even more so when you're rich. By this standard, the more good people gain money, the better the world gets.

There's plenty of proof that when women get money, they do good things with it. Dolly Parton has donated millions to scientific research and disaster relief. She also founded the Dollywood Foundation to support children's literacy, sending books to kids. Pop superstar Rihanna has funded initiatives that improve education and access to reproductive health services. Taylor Swift donated to local food banks at every stop on The Eras Tour and has donated millions to disaster relief efforts and animal welfare causes.

She also uses her massive platform to encourage fans to donate to local animal rescue organizations.

It's not just female celebrities who do good with their money. Ordinary, noncelebrity women leverage their resources to uplift communities and support meaningful causes every day. *Forbes* reported that women, in general, are more likely to give to charity as their incomes rise. This fact is backed by the "Women & Girls Index," which reports that women are more likely to donate to charity than men, and they are also more likely to give to organizations that support women and girls. TD Wealth reported that Canadian women's annual donations increased by 287% in one year, from $1.5 billion to $4.3 billion.

Once I finally started working on changing my relationship with money, I began to let a healthier money mindset flow in. I faced my monthly budget tracker with the attitude of, "It's empowering and fun to track my spending and see how much I can save," rather than, "It's terrifying and embarrassing to see how much I spent on donuts last month."

I began to make careful financial choices. I have launched businesses that helped me build my wealth and support the causes I love. I've donated proceeds from my launches to Black Lives Matter, the Heart and Stroke Foundation, and various animal sanctuaries. When filmmaker Rebecca Cappelli started crowdfunding to produce her documentary *Slay*, which exposes animal cruelty in the fashion industry, I was able to jump right in and add some funds to the cause. I want you to have this ability, too. I want more women to feel empowered to own their finances and enter their rich girl era.

Money isn't the enemy, so please stop feeling guilty for wanting mountains of wealth. Call it in and claim it. Stop saying, "I'm not good with money." You're an adult; learn. Stop thinking you're "bad" with money just because you weren't taught financial literacy in school. (Most of us weren't.) Also, you need to be bad at something before you become good at it. More good people need to become rich, wouldn't you agree?

Staying small, struggling, and believing you don't deserve it? That's the real trap. Say it out loud: "I love money! And money loves me!"

Entrepreneur Mindset Shift

If you've been raised to believe the only way to make money is to work a 9-to-5 until retirement, it's time for a major mindset shift. Starting today, vow to drop that nonsense and start thinking like an entrepreneur. An employee thinks, "I work, I get paid, I stop working, I stop getting paid," while an entrepreneur believes, "I build something once, and it pays me over and over again." That's the difference between surviving and thriving.

I must confess that traditional office jobs never worked for me. ADHD + misophonia + corporate life? Absolutely not. To begin with, my ADHD made it difficult because I couldn't force myself to be a "good employee" or sit in meetings when my brain simply does not function in rigid, structured environments.

On top of that, my misophonia, the intolerance of certain sounds, made it impossible. Misophonia is a neurological disorder where specific sounds trigger strong negative emotions like anger, disgust, and anxiety. For example, most people can hear others chewing food and be unbothered by it. Or they might find it a bit annoying, but they can still ignore it and get on with whatever they are doing. People with misophonia, however, can *not* tolerate the sound of it, regardless of how irrational it may be. While it's happening, a misophonia sufferer is sent into panicked fight-or-flight mode, and the turmoil the sound causes them is all-consuming. Our brains can't tell the difference between the unpleasant sound of someone eating and an actual physical threat. It feels like we are about to be *attacked*, making us feel compelled to run away immediately (usually in a silent, heart-pounding rage) even if we are completely normal, pleasant, chill people otherwise. As soon as the sound stops, we are back to normal.

My guess is that misophonia originates in some ancient survival instinct that was probably very helpful in early human days. Imagine you are a cave person, walking alone in the woods, and all of a sudden, you hear a twig snap behind you. In a split second, your adrenaline shoots from 0 to 100. Without hesitation, you are instantly ready to either run away from or karate chop a saber-toothed cat. Which sounds really badass. In modern times, as you might imagine, this is something that makes family meals, movie theaters, public transportation, and office jobs an internal personal hell. I couldn't focus in open-plan offices where every single sound made me want to scream and bolt from the room. People crunching on potato chips and rustling wrappers at their desks? THAT'S MOLOTOV COCKTAIL TIME.

Aside from the daily possibility of committing workplace arson, lifestyle-wise, the corporate grind just felt like a drag all around. I didn't want to have to change out of my cozy yoga pants in the morning for sensory-irritating work pants and a bra. Commuting on public transit to an office was not my idea of living my best life. The list went on. I needed a different way to make money. One where I could work how I wanted, when I wanted, without feeling like I was constantly failing at "normal" life. Online entrepreneurship was my saving grace. It let me leverage my skills, create wealth on my terms, and build a life that actually works for my brain. Working from home was the essential environment I needed to thrive. Once I made this a nonnegotiable, it stuck.

Thinking back to my childhood, the building blocks of entrepreneurship were always there, although I didn't know there was a word for it. At age seven, when I heard my school was having a bake sale fundraiser, I had a genius idea. On the day of the bake sale, I raided my piggy bank. I packed $10 worth of quarters into a Ziploc bag and headed to school. I used the money to buy out as many treats from the bake sale as I could. Each treat was ten cents. I then walked around to the other side of the playground, laid out some paper towels on the ground, and opened up shop. I resold the treats to kids for $1–2 each, and they sold out within minutes. When I came home from school, I plopped my bag of money on the coffee table in front of my mom. I was so excited to tell her what I'd done! I was so proud of myself. "Look, Mom, I resold cookies from the school bake sale and made all this money!"

To my surprise, she was not thrilled about this. She told me what I'd done was a little dishonest (I'd bought the goods fair and square, but I suppose the bake sale *was* a fundraiser). She made me donate the money back to the school. As instructed, I begrudgingly delivered the bag of cash to the Principal's office the next day. Despite this result, the embers of entrepreneurship had been lit in me, and there was no putting them out.

From that day on, I found ways to make money from every angle. When my mom rescued a malnourished horse that needed medical care, I pushed my bike up and down the beach, selling water bottles and pop to sunbathers to raise money for her vet bills. In high school, I bought cases of chocolate bars from Costco and sold them out of my locker to students as they returned from their midday marijuana sessions in the parking lot.

My sales strategy was simple:

- Pinpoint a desire (sunbathers are thirsty/stoners have the munchies).
- Identify a problem (they don't want to leave the beach/aren't allowed to skip class to go to a store)
- Sell them the solution, and make it so convenient, it's an easy yes.

This basic sales strategy still applies today. Of course, you can make it fancier nowadays with websites, ads, influencer marketing, and sales funnels. Yet, the basics still apply. Who is your customer? What desire do they have? What problem is stopping them from getting what they want? What product can you sell them to deliver this desire and solve their problem?

Get really clear on what your money goals are. Then ask yourself, "What sort of environment do I need so that I can hit those goals?" Plan it out today. Remember, the more money you attract in your life glow-up era, the more options and freedom you gain. The ultimate flex is the ability to walk away from anything that no longer serves you. It's about buying back your time and creating security for yourself and your loved ones. So, start talking about money. Start earning more. Start investing. Because wealth isn't just for "other people." It's for you, too.

Front of House

My first real job (aside from the occasional babysitting gig) was working at a bakery when I was a young teen. It was the summer, and my friend, Deanna, who was the same age as me, got hired at the same time. Somehow, despite our collective lack of life experience, we were trusted to open and close the bakery entirely on our own. No supervision. No adult oversight. Just two teenagers who were left in charge of an entire establishment. Looking back, I have no idea why anyone thought that was a good idea.

To be fair, Deanna and I were *mostly* responsible employees—during business hours, at least. But the moment we flipped the sign to "Closed," all bets were off. The back room became our personal concert venue. We'd blast Britney Spears, Eminem, and Sum 41 at full volume, tossing our T-shirts into the rafters and dancing on the tables in our bras. All while stuffing our faces with leftover Nanaimo bars as we attempted to clean the shop for the night. "In Too Deep" by Sum 41 was our backroom-table-dancing song of choice. It was a blast! On particularly slow days, we'd entertain ourselves by having full-on baguette sword fights with the stale bread.

Incredibly, we never got caught. Or maybe the owner just didn't care as long as the bakery looked spotless the next morning. Anyway, it was a fun part-time job.

The island we lived on was too small to have its own high school. So by eighth grade, all the high school age kids had to take a water taxi every morning to a different island, Salt Spring, where the nearest high school was located. In this regard, my high school experience was a bit unusual—waking up at the crack of dawn to catch a boat to school, spending the day on a completely different island from where we lived, and then racing back to the dock after class so we wouldn't miss the last boat home. Some mornings on the water taxi, I'd see orca whales passing by, and that alone made the early wake-ups feel worth it.

At first, the commute felt like an adventure, but by my second year, the novelty had worn off, and the daily trek started to feel like an exhausting time-suck. So when Deanna's mom decided to move to Salt Spring Island and offered to let me and a few of our other friends board at her place until we graduated, I didn't think twice.

Suddenly, I went from long, draining commutes to living in what was essentially a teenager-run household. Deanna's mom was out of town a lot, which meant that most of the time, we were just a handful of unsupervised teens with our own house to look after. We called it "Kid House," and it was exactly as chaotic as it sounds. There were always at least ten people visiting, climbing on the roof, and sledding down the stairs. There was never a dull moment. But despite the merry mayhem, those years in Kid House gave us our first real taste of independence. We had to grocery shop, cook, and make sure we got ourselves to school on time, and I wouldn't trade that for anything.

Throughout high school, I had a few different part-time jobs after moving on from the bakery. Each was equally weird for a teenage girl. Cleaning construction sites, laying insulation in crawl spaces, sitting in a boat writing down numbers while someone measured how high or low the water was that day, planting grapes at a winery, and it went on.

The most normal job I had as a teen was washing dishes and performing prep cook duties at a restaurant. I loved learning how to make fancy desserts there. Did you know a blowtorch is used to make the top of a crème brûlée crisp? As soon as I turned eighteen, however, they thrust me into the front of house (FOH), "You're a server now. Upsell things."

Block Party

More than a decade after closing my last tab, I still have PTSD nightmares from serving. Dreams where the restaurant is filling up with customers, and I'm the only worker on the floor, running around panicking, forgetting orders, and getting yelled at. Even though the job of waitressing is awful, working in restaurants is the kind of experience that everyone should do at least once. I often say, work in a restaurant long enough to hone your multitasking, sales, and teamwork skills, but not long enough to catch a cocaine habit.

I have to admit that it was serving jobs that opened my awareness of my ability to earn piles of cash quickly and abundantly and, in addition, they taught me a lot about sales strategy. Long before I ever closed a deal online, before I knew the ins and outs of digital marketing, before I built and sold websites, my first real sales training came from waitressing, a place few people would think to look.

When I waited tables at a popular lounge in Vancouver as a university student, like most young servers, I started off thinking my job was just delivering food and drinks and turning over tables enough times to maximize tips. Soon, I realized that the real money came from upselling. You see, the best servers aren't mere order takers; the gifted ones read every customer to strategically influence their experience. That means suggesting premium cocktails instead of house liquor, recommending appetizers that perfectly pair with entrées, and describing the dessert menu with as much swoonery as a long-haired man is described in a romance novel.

I learned to read people fast. Businessmen on expense accounts? Easy! They wanted top-shelf everything and expected a little tongue-in-cheek humor and teasing. Straight couples on a date? Sell them the reasonably priced bottle of wine, dote on the woman like she's the hottest person in the world, and acknowledge the man no more than necessary. Gay couples on a date? They want the best of the menu and their drinks fast, with a few self-deprecating jokes on the side. If they're both women, lightly flirt with each gal equally. If they're both men, well, surprisingly, the same tip applies. A table of indecisive tourists? Guide them like a seasoned food critic, and then let them have their peace.

The real aha moment came when I realized that my customers at the restaurant weren't just diners; they were also potential clients for my side hustle. I had been dabbling in website design on the side and teaching myself to code. One night, I was making casual conversation with some regulars who came in for happy hour a few times a week, and it came up. They ran businesses, worked in finance, and spent their evenings at the bar swapping stories about their work. "Wait, you build websites? We need one. Can you do it?" Just like that, I had my first client.

After that, I started bringing it up website design more intentionally. I'd subtly ask customers about their work, listen for any signs that they needed an online presence, and then I'd mention that I built websites. It was the easiest pitch in the world! No pressure, just a friendly conversation over dinner. I started carrying a stack of business cards in my server pouch, ready to slip to potential clients at any time. Over time, I landed multiple freelance clients from my restaurant job.

I also picked up a surprising amount of financial wisdom in that restaurant job from a few regulars who worked in finance. One guy once told me, "If you want to experience real wealth, don't just work for money; put your money to work for you. Allow your money to make more money." He went on to explain investing and passive income.

Another customer told me, "The smartest business move is to find a way to get paid while you sleep." While another promised, "If you can carry three plates at once, you can handle three income streams." At the time, I didn't fully grasp the weight of their advice, but those conversations planted the seeds for what I would later come to know very well.

One day, while polishing cutlery, my boss let me know that the company that owned our restaurant also owned the one across the street. I was surprised to learn this information. From the outside, everyone assumed the two places were rivals, competing for the same customers. She revealed, "If you're going to have competition, you might as well own the competition. That way, no matter where the customer goes, the money still lands in your pocket. *Own the block.*"

That piece of advice stuck with me. Years later, when I started acquiring businesses, I applied the same strategy. Instead of trying to dominate a niche with just one brand, I'd buy multiple sites in the same space, competitor brands, essentially, and run them anonymously. That way, no matter which "choice" a customer made, they were still choosing me. I do this across multiple niches, too. It is one of the smartest ways to diversify income streams, and it all started with a lesson I learned slinging drinks as a waitress.

Looking back, I realize that through those grueling shifts, while I thought I was wasting away my life in a dead-end job, I was learning a lot. The restaurant world unknowingly trained me in sales psychology, customer service, networking, and negotiation. It showed me that the best way to sell is not by being pushy. Instead, it's about understanding what people need and offering them a solution. So, if you think your current job has nothing to do with your future business, think again. The skills to acquire are there. You just have to recognize them.

How to Sell Things Without Giving People the Ick

Many new entrepreneurs find sales and marketing challenging. They often think it's about convincing people to buy things they don't really need, which should never be the case. Good marketing is just helping people make decisions. Your job is not to convince people to do anything.

You may think this sounds crazy, but your job is not to sell, either! Your job is to solve a problem. Your content shows your audience how a product can help them with their problems. It's all about guiding them to the best decision *for them*, not pressuring them into one. The right people for your offer will be happy to get their hands on it.

No one wants to come off like a pushy used car salesman. It's uncomfortable when you feel like you're shoving a deal at someone while they search for a way out. Also, people can smell desperation. That panicky "please buy from me, or I won't be able to pay rent" energy? It does the opposite of what you want. It makes people run.

I learned this lesson early on, entirely by accident, back when I was waitressing and freelancing as a website designer. I had just started offering my design services but had no clue how to sell myself. My instinct was to try way too hard, oversell, and babble on about how I was "super available" and "willing to work within any budget." Translation: I was desperate and would take whatever scraps were thrown at me.

By now, at the restaurant, I had perfected my casual mention that I wasn't just a professional tray carrier, that I built websites and sales pages. Eventually, I learned a critical sales lesson. One time, after my usual subtle pitch of my freelance business, the customer perked up and said, "Oh, we actually need one. Do you have a portfolio?"

Instead of launching into "Pick me! Pick me! I can start right now! I'll even give you a discount!" mode, I decided to play it cool. I shrugged and said, "Yeah, I've done a few sites for small businesses. What kind of website are you looking for?"

I let him do the talking. Instead of convincing him, I let him convince himself. By the end of dinner, he was asking me how soon I could start.

That moment taught me a critical sales lesson. People don't want to be sold to. They want to feel like they're making the best decision for themselves. The easiest way to sell something is to detach from the outcome.

Even if you are absolutely not feeling cool, act like you are. Even if you really need this sale, act like you don't. Not in a douchey, I'm-too-good-for-you kind of way, but in an "I'm a professional, and if we're a good fit, great; if not, no problem" way.

It is such a powerful play when you can shift your mindset from "I need to convince them to buy" to "I'm just helping them make the best choice for them." That's how you turn the act of selling into a casual conversation, not a high-stakes transaction. The funny thing is, the moment you stop needing the sale so badly, that's when people start wanting to buy from you.

If you offer services, here's another powerful mindset tip that does wonders: Stop presenting yourself as a freelancer and start presenting yourself as a consultant. A freelancer is a struggling, desperate Jacklyn-of-all-trades who will take any discounted rate just to get by. On the other hand, a consultant is a professional who solves her client's problems, is in high demand, and is highly paid *on a retainer* for her skills. Those two have very different energies. Can you feel it? Your potential clients can feel it. Pick the one that puts you in the power seat. I love this for you.

The Power of Words

Did you know that your brain believes everything you tell it, whether it's true or not? Good or bad? Yep! Your little CPU is basically a zealous intern who takes everything you say as gospel and then runs around trying to prove you right.

Tell yourself, "I'm broke," and your brain goes, "Got it! Let's make sure you see insufficient funds notifications, unexpected expenses, and missed financial opportunities everywhere." Suddenly, you're overdrawing your account and ignoring your bank statements like they're a lame ex texting, "You up?"

This is science! Our brains have something called a reticular activating system (RAS). Our RAS filters out unnecessary information in our surroundings so that we can focus on what's important at that moment. Whatever you tell your brain, your RAS will hear and interpret it as being important to you. Then, it will constantly look for signals and guide you toward evidence that proves it. It doesn't process whether your words are a lie or the truth. It can't differentiate between what you perceive as actually happening or what you imagine. So this is why it makes 100% sense only to tell yourself *positive things* that you want to happen! *Words. Freaking. Matter.* Your brain is listening. It's taking notes and actively shaping your reality based on what you keep reinforcing. All negative money talk has got to go.

Here are some money-related statements that you need to stop saying or thinking (like yesterday) and the positive swaps to say instead:

- **"I'm broke."** DELETE this word from your memory and replace it with, "Money is flowing to me in expected and unexpected ways." Even if right now, that's just in the form of finding $5 in your jacket pocket.

- **"I can't afford that."** Instead, say, "That's not in my budget right now, but I'm working toward it." See the difference? One shuts down possibility; the other keeps the door open.

- **"I suck at saving money."** Not anymore! Replace this with, "I'm learning how to manage and grow my money every day." You don't suck; you're just learning, and that's how people get better at things

- **"I am terrible with money."** Nope! Now you say, "I am becoming more financially savvy every day." Rewire your brain to believe it, and your actions will follow.

- **"Ugh, money stresses me out."** No, it doesn't! Repeat,

"I am in control of my finances, and I'm figuring it out."

What if you could start treating your brain like your best friend, whom you only want the best for? You'd never tell your best friend, "Ugh, you're the worst at everything. You'll never be successful. You're so broke, it's pathetic." So why are you talking to yourself that way? Talk to yourself like you expect good things to happen and hype yourself up. Because the second you start saying, "Money is everywhere and always there for me," instead of "I'm always broke," your brain will go, "Got it! Let's find some proof of that."

I want you to be *very* literal with the words you say to yourself. Don't make your brain read between the lines. As a neurodivergent person, I tend to follow instructions on a literal, face-value level already. Sometimes, this has put me in hot water, especially back when I was an employee.

As a young twenty-something, I was excited to land my first office job, supporting the marketing department of the restaurant where I worked. Making the move from FOH to Head Office was something that upper management would like to have everyone believe is important. I worked directly under the marketing manager, Steven, helping him with planning events and booking talent. I was eager to please and wanted to do a great job in the new role.

When I was assigned to projects that allowed me to write, design, or think creatively, I was in my element and did a great job. But in interpersonal situations, sometimes I struggled to understand much of what my coworkers meant by what they said. Sure, I had learned to gauge my customers as a server, but this was a whole new ball game. I was also super young and simply didn't understand yet that there are many unspoken things that you are just supposed to know.

Although I had a little bit of marketing experience at the time, I was still very green in the corporate world. “Chelsea, I need you to go to the wine event at the Conference Centre today and distribute my business card,” Steven told me when I arrived at the office one morning.

“Okay!” I smiled, accepting the stack of business cards from him. Float some cards around a wine event. Sounds fun and easy!

Off I went. When I arrived at the event, I immediately got to work distributing the business cards. Steven had given me about 150 of them. I saw that people were leaving their cards on a table by the front desk. Perfect. I placed a small stack of Steven’s cards there. Then, I went to each booth and placed a small stack of cards on the table in each one. I also put some stacks on the dining area tables and in the wine tasting area. Within thirty minutes, I’d unloaded them all.

The next day, Steven asked me how it went.

“Great! I distributed all of them,” I nodded.

He looked surprised. “Wow! All of them?”

“Yep! Every last one,” I replied with a smile, knowing I had done a good job.

“That’s awesome!” he cheered. “You can leave the contacts’ business cards on my desk, and I’ll follow up with them.”

Contacts’ business cards? What contacts’ business cards? My heart skipped a beat. *He never told me to get people’s business cards.*

He saw that I looked horrified. “You did make some good vendor connections, yes?”

Uh-oh. Was I supposed to actually *talk* to people? Steven only told me to distribute his cards. He didn't say I had to talk to or exchange cards with people. The vision of me confidently going from booth to booth, engaging with no one, flashed into my mind's eye.

"Uh...I, I didn't get anyone's cards. I'm so sorry," I stuttered, realizing I'd made a huge rookie mistake by taking Steven's "distribute business cards" instructions way too literally. I had walked around the venue like a business card fairy, sprinkling them on tables and window ledges. I might have even slipped a few into the bathroom stalls, like, "For a good time, call my boss."

I hadn't read between the lines. What Steven meant, of course, was to talk to people, shake hands, and exchange cards. Make human contact. Oops. He actually wanted me to go and network and make connections with wine reps. *Why not just say that, then?*

Steven frowned, "What wine brands did you pursue? Do you remember the names of the brand reps?"

Time to think on your feet, Chelsea. Do what you do best, girl.

"Oh, I made a contact list for you," I lied.

His frown did a little cartwheel into a smile. "Perfect."

"I'll have it emailed to you by lunch," I assured him confidently, "I just need to organize it into a spreadsheet. I won't torture you with my handwriting." Wow, I'm good.

I then ran to the bathroom, locked myself in a stall, and frantically looked up the wine event on my phone to see if any of the vendors were listed. Fortunately, there were dozens of wine brands, rep names, and sponsor names listed. I then looked up each one on social media to see who had posted photos of themselves at the event, tracked faces to names on their company's associated

LinkedIn profiles, and did some Googling, noting any email addresses. I then emailed the list to myself and headed back to my desk, where I compiled my work into a spreadsheet. Somehow, this passed, and no one was the wiser.

Although I avoided embarrassment with some quick-thinking ingenuity, the lesson I learned from this was bigger. See, this taught me just how wired our brains are for survival and success. Remember, your brain believes every word you tell it and works tirelessly to show you proof. If you're anything like me (neurodivergent, can get laser-focused on a task to a fault, or someone who takes language very literally) the way the RAC functions can be both your superpower and stumbling block.

On the one hand, it's incredible for manifestation and breaking into new healthy habits. I tell my brain, "I'm building a seven-figure business," or "I don't get drunk anymore," and my brain's like, "Got it. On it." I don't need a manifestation coach or new moon rituals. I just need to say it like it's already true, and my brain gets to work proving me right. On the other hand, there are those times when it works against me, like how I took Steven's "distribute business cards" instruction at face value. I wasn't given specific instructions about what my boss actually wanted, so I only focused on the words I was told. I only did the bare minimum, in what I understood from those words.

If we don't give our brains specific instructions about what we want, we can't expect to get the results we want. The more clearly we communicate with ourselves, the more likely we are to actually get the outcome we mean to ask for. Since our brains are going to take what we tell them literally, then we better leverage that by feeding it the exact narrative we want it to believe.

So now, when I talk to myself, I talk like someone who has already closed the deal, landed the dream client, or sold out the course. I don't wait until it's "real." I make it real in my imagination and get into the flow, *the feeling* of it being my reality now. My brain doesn't know the difference between a fact and a fabrication, and neither does yours.

The lesson? When speaking to yourself, be specific, be kind, and claim what it is you want. Make it clear with no room for misinterpretation. Then, don't spend another second focusing on the things you don't want.

Want one more example of a time I took words way too literally and looked silly? At twenty-one, I was interviewing for a job, and everything was going great at first. The interviewer appeared to like me, and I thought I had it in the bag. Then she asked her last question: "If you could be anything, what would you be? Dream big!"

Without hesitation, I confidently replied, "I'd be able to fly! That would be awesome!" Suddenly, the energy in the room shifted. She had an odd look on her face and acted a bit weird as she ended the meeting and sent me on my way. It wasn't until I was a block down the street that I realized she had meant what would I be *professionally*. Like, for a career. Sorry, not sorry. I don't dream of labor.

Loud Money Literacy

Now that we are breaking down all that "good girl" programming, it's time to start talking about money like it's just another Tuesday. Women are often taught that talking about money is tacky, unladylike, or "just not our thing." Meanwhile, men have no problem discussing their salaries, negotiating raises, and openly admitting they want to be rich. And guess what? That's one reason why they make more.

I want you to get really comfortable with money so you can start earning and keeping more of it and making sure it grows. The harsh reality is women still make less than men for the same work. The Pew Research Center states that in 2024, women earned an average of 85% of what men earned. We're not just paid less; we're promoted less, funded less, and conveniently left out of the rooms where deals happen. The National Partnership for Women & Families found that women employed in the United States lose a combined total of almost $1.7 trillion every year due to this wage gap.

So, how can women close the wage gap? Pay transparency! *You need to start talking about money.* Loudly. Confidently. Without shame. If you are an employee, discuss your salary with your coworkers. I mean it. Ask your coworkers what they make. I know, I know. You've been trained since birth never to ask someone about their salary. Do it anyway. Because guess what? Keeping salary talk hush-hush only benefits those who want to keep you underpaid.

Wouldn't you want to know if Dwerpo in accounting is making $20K more than you for the same job?

Make your salary and future with your company normal topics of discussion with your boss. Most women wait to be "noticed" for their hard work. Ha! As if a boss just sits at their desk, monitoring your progress progress, thinking, "Wow, you know what? I should give her more money." Um...they're not. *You have to make the ask.*

If you're underpaid at your job, say something. And if they don't fix it, find a place that will pay you more. The truth is that the people making the most money are not necessarily the most intelligent, hardworking, or even the most deserving. They simply had the audacity to ask for more.

Also, talk to your friends about investing, wealth-building, and business. Why are we still whispering about how much we earn from our investments or how much we charge for our services? Let your girls in on the financial tea. Make money and investing a normal topic of discussion in your circle.

If you're freelancing, consulting, or otherwise already in business, discuss pricing with other business owners, too. Stop guessing what to charge for your products and services. Join a Mastermind group to talk about pricing and money with other entrepreneurs. I host a community for business owners where transparent money conversations are the norm. Women from all walks of life and all stages of business, from experts to total newbies, share their advice openly in our group. I invite you to get in on the conversation at HerPaperRoute.com/join.

Women are often made to feel guilty for wanting wealth while being expected to work harder, prove more, accept less, and somehow remain grateful for the scraps. Meanwhile, men are exchanging handshakes over raises and investment opportunities left and right. The reality? Waiting for approval, recognition, or "fairness" is a losing game, which is why owning your own business is the ultimate power move. It lets you set your own rates, make your own rules, and put yourself into rooms and opportunities otherwise unavailable to you.

So here are your new money mantras:

- Wanting more doesn't make me greedy. It makes me aligned for growth.
- I'm allowed to want financial freedom.
- I openly say, "I love my rich life," and "I am rich," without shame."

Next, know that a paycheck from your employer should not be your only source of income. Because if it is, you are one corporate layoff away from financial turmoil. The goal you need to make a priority is to earn money from multiple sources, so you're never relying on just one. If you don't already have one, start a side hustle (freelancing, digital products, coaching, or consulting). You have skills; monetize them. Join the creator economy. It's booming! You don't need any qualifications. Simply start creating content, and boom, you're in the creator economy. Content creation is a huge business, and people are making money on blogs, YouTube, social media, and newsletters.

Don't stop there. Make your money pay you more money back; in other words, it is essential to invest and own revenue-generating assets. If your money is sitting in a savings account, it's losing value. (Inflation is a thief; stop texting him.) *You need to invest.* You can invest in stocks, TFSAs (tax-free savings accounts), retirement accounts, real estate, digital real estate, and more.

My preference is digital real estate—websites, to be exact. Websites are revenue-generating assets that can earn passive income. Website investing (aka buying, growing, and selling websites) is my favorite way to earn money in the creator economy. I can gush all about it to anyone who will listen. The kinds of websites I own primarily earn money through ad revenue, affiliate marketing, digital products, and brand deals. Websites can also sell services, physical products, memberships, and anything else someone can dream up. They're like rental properties but online.

I'll go into more detail about website investing later in this book, but basically, it involves:

- Buying a website that is already making money.
- Growing it (more traffic, better monetization).
- Selling it for a profit later.

This is precisely why I founded Niche Investor. To provide a place for women to buy and sell websites. It's a platform that gives creators options and more ways to build wealth.

Above all, if you haven't yet, prioritize getting serious about your financial independence. Real power is never having to depend on anyone else for money. I don't care if you're married, engaged, or living with someone who swears they "got you." *Have. Your. Own. Money.* Always have your own bank account. Always have your own savings and investments. Always have multiple revenue streams of *your own*.

Because when life throws you a curve ball (divorce, a job loss, or an emergency), you don't want to be stuck financially dependent on someone else, whether they're an employer, a partner, or family. Take control of your money

Your Daily Money Mindset Glow-Up Plan

If you want to build wealth, attract opportunities, and stop ugly-crying every time you check your bank account, you need to start treating your money mindset like a muscle. You can't just read about mindset once and expect instant results. You have to *train* a healthy mindset. How? Through small healthy habits, daily. Here's a simple, effective daily plan to help you shift your money mindset, build confidence around finances, and start making (and keeping) more money.

Morning: Set the Tone for Abundance

Start the day with a money affirmation. Say it aloud, write it down, or repeat it while brushing your teeth. "I am great with money." "Money loves me and is always flowing to me." "I am worthy of limitless wealth."

Check in with your accounts. Look at your bank and other accounts every day. Awareness is power. Even if they're not where you want them to be, you can't grow what you don't track. Keep a budget spreadsheet to watch your savings grow.

Take one income-generating action. Ask yourself: "What's one thing I can do today to move my finances forward?" Send an invoice. Follow up with a potential client. Research a new income stream. Raise your rates. Invest in something. Sell something. Open up Canva and create a new digital product. Do *something*.

Afternoon: Reset Your Money Mindset

Reframe one negative money belief. Whenever a limiting thought pops up during your day, reframe and rewrite it immediately. For example, if the thought, "I'll never make enough," comes to mind, correct yourself and say, "I will always make enough because I am making smart financial decisions now that will prosper." Or, when you think, "Rich people are greedy," go to the positive spin of, "I love seeing rich people prosper from their money moves; it's inspiring and shows me what is possible for me, too!" Instead of telling yourself, "I'm just not good with money," say, "I am learning to manage and grow my money daily." Do this consistently, and your brain will start believing the new, healthy thought patterns instead of the old ones.

Talk about money (out loud!). Let conversations about money be normal in your daily life. Ask a friend what they charge for freelance work. Discuss investing strategies with someone. Share a financial win with your community. The more we talk about money, the more it allows other women to feel confident sharing their money journeys, too.

Evening: Set Yourself Up for Long-Term Wealth

Track your wins. Before bed, write down one positive money action you took today. Saved $5? Write it down. Got paid for something? Write it down. Finally asked for that raise? WRITE. IT. DOWN. Money confidence builds when you acknowledge your progress.

Visualize your financial future like it's already happening. Close your eyes and picture your wealthiest, most financially free self. Where do you live? How much is in your bank account? What does your business/career look like? How do you feel waking up stress-free about money? This is training your brain to normalize financial success.

The Money Mindset Glow-Up Plan is how you prioritize your commitment to improving your relationship with money. Follow this plan for thirty days, and watch how your money mindset (and bank account) shift.

4

Breaking Up with Your Old Life

Your past self deserves for you to see yourself as someone who is powerful, capable, and whole. For this glow-up to happen, you need to upgrade your life now and even step into a new identity. Breaking up with your old life isn't about scorning who you used to be. It's about graduating from her.

I like to think of my past self as a younger sister who was just trying to figure it out. She made some mistakes. Still, that past version of you also had dreams, kept hoping, and held onto something, even when she didn't know how to get there. Yes, you are going to have to expel some of the bad habits and unnecessary baggage you picked up along the way, but you can do it with love.

The reason why shifting your habits, environment, and identity matters so much in your Glow-Up Plan is that the best way to respect the old you is to become the person she always needed you to be. You change your habits because your past self deserved better than what you settled for back then.

It's not necessary to hate where you came from to build something better; you just need to love yourself enough to go after more. So, let's explore the themes of environment, habits, and identity and their impact on your glow-up.

Environment

If you've ever felt stuck, uninspired, or like you're spinning in circles instead of moving toward your goals, let me ask you a question: What's surrounding you right now? And I don't just mean physically (though let's be real, your home office might need a glow-up, too). I mean, what are you surrounding yourself with, who are you talking to, and what's feeding your brain on a daily basis? Because your environment either supports your success or silently sabotages you.

Your brain is taking notes every second of the day. If you're spending your time with broke, negative, excuse-making people who complain about life but never take action? Your brain absorbs that energy. If you're constantly listening to content that makes you feel inadequate? Your brain files that under "reasons I should stay small and scared." If your social media feed is nothing but other people's success stories that actually make you feel left behind? Your brain will convince you you're already too late. What you consume, hear, and surround yourself with shapes your mindset, whether you realize it or not.

There was a time in my early twenties when my lifestyle was tragic. I mean toxic, stagnant, a black hole of no personal growth. I hadn't read a book in I don't know how long. I wasn't consuming or creating anything remotely positive. I wasn't learning, growing, evolving—anything. It was shortly after I returned to Vancouver from my stint in Hollywood as Seo-Yeon's third child.

At the time, I worked at an office as a marketing coordinator by day and at a nightclub as a bartender by night. If you've ever worked in the nightlife industry, you'll know that in that business, someone's entire existence becomes a revolving door of late nights, bad decisions, and short-lived friendships. I was either behind the bar serving drinks or on the other side drinking them. Every day. Day job shift, night job shift, after-party, sleep, repeat.

While everyone else my age was building a career, learning new skills, and making progress in life, I had pressed pause on my own development. Even my day job kept me in the void because it was event marketing for...the nightclub where I bartended! I look back now and realize that it was as though I just stepped out of society.

I didn't know what was happening in pop culture. I couldn't tell you what movies or TV shows were trending. I had no idea what was happening in the world, in business, in anything that actually mattered. The only thing I knew was when I had to be at work, which customers tipped well, and which after-party was worth attending. My creativity had vanished, too, and for those years, I didn't create, draw, write, or design anything.

Ugh, but here's the real kicker: I didn't even realize how long I had been falling behind. When your environment is full of people doing the same thing, it feels normal. That is, until one day in 2012 when I realized just how *not cool* I had let things get.

I was going to meet Jane, my old friend from university, for lunch and was excited to catch up with her after not seeing her for over a year. Little did I know that the lunch date would be *just* the violent shake I needed at that toxic time in my life. See, Jane was thriving, enjoying her career and making art. She wasn't involved in the party scene at all the way I was. She asked me about what I was working on (nothing) and if I still made art (nope). All I could think to talk about was club-kid nightlife gossip. Yawn.

Jane shrugged, "You're so creative. It's a shame you aren't creating anything anymore."

We sat at the restaurant, and reality started to sink in. Jane, my beautiful, vibrant, remarkably talented friend, had creativity-focused and wholesome topics to discuss. Everything I used to love talking to her about. Yet, that day, I had zero to contribute to the conversation. And she noticed it, too.

"Are you okay? I don't think you are." She sighed with deep sincerity. "You seem like you party a lot, which isn't like you.'

I opened my mouth, ready to give some surface-level excuse. Instead, choosing to be real, I nodded and admitted, "Yeah. You aren't wrong."

She shook her head. "Chels, you rarely even drank in university. Now, I'm worried about you."

The look in her eyes said everything. She wasn't judging me. *She felt bad for me*. Which, it turns out, feels worse!

Finally, it hit me. While my peers were starting businesses, nurturing their creativity, and moving up in life, I had regressed. And that realization was painful. I had wasted years in a bubble of stagnation, doing little for my life. While surrounding myself with people who also weren't thinking about the future, weren't growing, and weren't doing anything but killing time.

After lunch, I walked home with a heavy feeling in my heart. I was so caught up in a shitty lifestyle. Even if I knew how to untangle myself from it, would I even bother trying? Would it even matter at this point? *That's my cue!* The universe giggled, unbeknownst to me.

Upheaval

The uncomfortable feeling lingered for some time after my lunch with Jane. I was living with my friend Lana in a one-bedroom apartment in Vancouver. Lana was a stand-up comedian and one of the funniest people I'd ever met. A Gemini like me, our birthdays were only days apart. It always felt like there was some out-of-this-world bond that connected us. Like we were meant to meet and be there for each other at that time in our lives.

Interestingly, Lana's dad was an editorial cartoonist like my grandpa. We found out that before we were born, her dad and my grandpa would hang out, fostering a friendship of their own. Long afterward, when Lana and I met, it was unconnected to our families. That kind of unexplainable synchronicity was just too perfect.

Lana and I shared a bunk bed in the bedroom of our apartment at first. I had the bottom bunk; she had the top. It was a funny, whimsical living arrangement that worked for about a year. Then, when she got a boyfriend, the bunk bed got dismantled, and I moved my mattress into the living room to give Lana and her boyfriend some privacy when he'd stay over. Which, I'd noticed had become more and more frequent lately.

One night, I returned home from my bartending shift, exhausted, only to walk straight into a plot twist I (somehow) didn't see coming. Lana and her boyfriend told me that they had decided that they wanted to live there, just the two of them. Apparently, I was not part of that vision.

I was pissed, not at either one of them specifically, but because having someone else decide your next move for you stings. However, underneath the initial frustration, I had this weird feeling that this was exactly the push I needed. Deep down, I already knew I needed to move on.

When I arrived at my office job the following morning, one of my managers asked me to send him a list of everything I did there. A list of my daily, weekly, and monthly duties. That's odd, I thought and went ahead and sent him the full list of all my activities, like an idiot. Without realizing it, I had just provided a perfectly organized job description for my replacement.

A couple of days later, I was brought into the boardroom and told that the company was making changes, and my job had been made redundant. I was no longer needed and was being laid off. The person I trained as an intern would be taking over. *Oh, shit.*

"You can still bartend at our venues," they nodded, as if that were some kind of prize.

"You can still bartend at our venues," as if that was some kind of prize.

All I could think about as I walked home that day was that I should have saved more money. *Why did I spend every paycheck like I'd always have this job?*

The more it set in, the more I realized just how risky it really is to be an employee. You have no control; you can lose your job at any moment. This layoff radicalized me and set me on a whole new path to becoming someone who would learn to build an emergency fund. *I will never not have savings ever again,* I promised myself with determination.

But for now, I needed to find a new apartment because Lana and her boyfriend were trying to play house, and I was cramping their style.

As I started apartment hunting, I quickly realized that staying in Vancouver sans a roommate would not be easy, especially now that I was down one of my two jobs. Vancouver's rents are a well-known bad joke; though, places to live outside of the city were slightly more affordable. Maybe I should move to a different town? Heck, I had lived in Hollywood on my own; I could make that work. I had no idea what I was getting into. Still, something in me whispered, "This might be exactly what you need."

When I looked inward and held a mirror up to myself, it was too obvious that I needed to get the hell out of Vancouver again, not just physically but mentally, emotionally, and lifestyle-wise. I had been stuck in the party loop—drinking, late nights, seeing the same people, having the same conversations, feeling the same feeling of being stuck in place while everyone else was moving forward.

I had to admit that a change of environment could be good.

Moving Out

Even outside of Vancouver, rental options were scarce. Then, like a love note from my spirit guides, I came across an ad: "Office space for rent. 24-hour access." Hmm, a light bulb started flickering in my brain. Could I live in an office building for a little while until I figured things out? There's desperate...and then there's "I'll just live in an office space" desperate.

It was an old two-story walk-up-style building. The offices were on the second floor. Six suites. Each office was private, with its own locking door. There was a shared coffee room and bathroom. My suite came with a desk and mini fridge and had a window looking out at the mountains. It wasn't bad at all. And I could afford it.

"I'll mostly be here at night," I told the manager. There, see, I'm not lying to anyone.

"That's fine," he shrugged.

So, I took the leap, signed a lease, put my belongings into storage, and moved into an office building in a city where I knew no one. I only brought the essentials (my laptop and two couch cushions to serve as a bed), and for the next few months, I lived in a literal office. The other offices on the floor were rented out to people whom I'd rarely see. Everyone had their own space and pretty much kept to themselves. No one suspected a thing.

Suddenly, I had zero distractions. No drinking buddies calling me to go out. No familiar bars pulling me back into old habits. No excuses. Everything started shifting for the better. I took on some freelance work designing websites and flyers for local musicians and business owners. I spent my days visiting cafes and parks in my new city, going on little solo dates with myself. Finally, I began reading books again.

And, gosh darn it, wouldn't you know it? I started to feel my creativity coming back. I found myself learning new skills, and thanks to spending time with my new musician friends, I discovered that I enjoy making music, too. I'm not trained in any instrument specifically, but my neurodivergent brain hears music in my head constantly. It's easy for me to find sounds, loops, and noises and to arrange them in a way that makes sense. Well, to me, anyway, I'm not sure how it sounds to anyone else. Soon, making beats and experimental soundscapes became my favorite creative outlet.

Most importantly, I started to feel like myself again. It felt like I was finally rejoining society instead of existing in the nightlife bubble I had been trapped in for years. At night, I'd arrive home, lock myself in my suite, shut the blinds, open my laptop, and get to work. I'd curl up under the desk on my couch cushion bed and quietly exist in my office suite speakeasy. Usually, I was the only person in the building that late. Once in a while, someone would be in the office across the hall, but no one was ever there overnight other than me. I'd work all night on my startup and creative projects, get a few hours of sleep, and then sneak out in the early hours of the morning before the manager arrived. This way, he wouldn't suspect that I'd been sleeping there.

I didn't know it at the time, but all of that fiddling around and experimenting laid the foundation for my future business, HerPaperRoute, even though it seemed like I was just trying to get a few sales for my dropshipping store. It wasn't a million-dollar empire (not even close!). It wasn't even my forever business. But it was the best crash course in entrepreneurship I could have asked for. It was during those late nights at the office, as I pretended I didn't live there, that I learned how to sell online. I learned how to build a brand. I figured out what works, what doesn't, and how to pivot. I practiced, failed, and practiced again without pressure.

I applied much of what I had learned at my previous marketing job to my own pursuits. Having written marketing emails for that company, I tested the same strategies for my email list. Applying website optimization techniques in my previous job, I tweaked them for my store. And knowing how to run social media ads helped me grow my audience. By the time I launched HerPaper-Route a few years later, my time to reach success was cut in half. Why? Because I had already made my beginner mistakes in the training ground of that first business.

That move out of Vancouver, as random and chaotic as it felt at the time, became the reset button my life desperately needed. Looking back now, I realize that getting pushed out of the apartment and the office job weren't the setbacks I thought they were. It was my escape. The universe wasn't punishing me. It was forcing me to level up. Changing your environment changes your future. If you don't like where your life is going, look around. Who you spend time with, what you consume, and what you prioritize will shape everything. I know because I wasted years in the wrong place.

For months, I lived the weirdest double life. Part startup entrepreneur, part professional squatter. And honestly? It was kind of genius. I showered at the gym down the road like a high-functioning adult (who also technically didn't have a shower at "home"). I never left dishes in the communal coffee room. I kept my belongings out of sight so my "workspace" looked professionally minimalist instead of questionably residential. I got really good at blending in. Those months of covert office dwelling changed me. I learned to adapt and survive with less. Most importantly, I realized that when you truly want something, you find a way to make it happen.

If you are waiting for more money, more time, or more "perfect" conditions before you start, you're wasting time. Start with what you have. Be scrappy. Get creative. Find a way. Resourcefulness is the shortcut to success.

Evidence

You know what used to be one of my toxic traits? Seeing someone absolutely thriving, whether in business or life, and immediately taking it as a personal attack. Like, how dare they be successful, happy, and glowing while I'm over here floundering and crying on my degree?

I used to think someone else's success meant the universe was teasing me for my shortcomings. As if it was holding up a giant flashing sign that said, "LOOK AT ALL THE WAYS YOU'RE

FAILING!" (Rude.) Instead of celebrating others, I'd secretly feel jealous, insecure, and convinced that their wins somehow meant I was losing.

I was twenty-eight when I moved into the office building on the down-low. Although I was putting in effort to learn new skills and revive my creativity, I wasn't out of the hole yet. I still had no real career prospects, no brilliant business ideas, and no sustainable revenue streams. Oh, and no serious love interests, either.

To go even deeper, I felt the big, scary 30 looming over me, that invisible deadline society slaps on women like an expiration date on milk. Did I even want a serious partner, ever? I wasn't sure, but society and *The Bachelor* sure were making me feel like I should have the option lined up by now. (Side note: You do not shrivel up and die after thirty. Shockingly, life keeps going. And even gets better! Who knew? Also, you don't have to get married. There are a million reasons why women benefit greatly by *not* marrying and instead choosing to stay single.) But at the time, I was spiraling.

One night, I returned "home" to my office space from yet another waste-of-makeup date, where the idea of anything serious was so not on the person's radar. Sad, exhausted, and feeling utterly defeated with where I was in life, I opened Facebook. And it was like a highlight reel of everything I didn't have. Engaged friends, people from high school closing on their first homes, promotions, and dreamy vacation pics in Santorini. Happy women who look like sun-kissed goddesses in their perfectly lit selfies. Meanwhile, there I was, secretly living in an office with no career or love prospects, lying on the floor, sobbing, and deep in a full-blown self-pity spiral.

I'm so behind. I missed my chance. It's too late for me. I have no future.

Oh, woman, how wrong I was. Because, eventually (not that night on the floor in my puddle of tears, but eventually), I realized something game-changing. Their success? Their beauty? Their achievements? None of it takes away from what's mine. In fact, it's proof that what I want is possible.

When you change your mindset, you realize that seeing someone absolutely killing it in their career, business, or personal life isn't the universe mocking you. Rather, the universe is saying, "Hey, look! This can happen for you, too!" Now, when I see someone thriving, I don't feel small; I feel inspired. I see successful women as proof that my goals aren't crazy. I see beautiful women and think, Wow, what a masterpiece! I'm going to try my eyeliner like that. Instead of, Wow, I'm a potato.

I genuinely celebrate people's wins because I know that success is not a limited resource; someone's success isn't a threat to mine. And honestly, this mindset shift has been everything. When you stop seeing others as competition and start seeing what they're doing as evidence that your dreams are valid, life gets a whole lot more exciting. You're being shown what's possible.

I know, it's hard to see a silver lining when you're in the mud. I bet you've been there. You're scrolling through Instagram, minding your own business, when—bam! Someone you know just bought their dream house, landed a six-figure brand deal, or casually jetted off to Italy again. And suddenly, it feels personal, as if the universe is throwing success in your face as a reminder that you're still stuck in the F-around-and-find-out phase.

Your brain starts looping. Why not me? What am I doing wrong? Is my vision board broken? You try to be happy for them, yet deep down, there's that little pang of envy. And then comes the worst part: guilt for feeling envious in the first place.

What if I told you that desiring more for yourself doesn't mean you're falling behind? What if it's actually proof that you're on the right track? Have you ever seen someone accomplish something and felt a gut feeling, like you know you could do that too? That's not jealousy. That's alignment. That's the universe nudging you, saying, "Hey, you're in the right lane. Explore this interest."

Now, every time you see someone thriving, instead of thinking, That should be me, flip the script: That COULD be me. Others' success is living proof that the things you dream about aren't just possible; they're happening. Right now. In real life. And if it's happening for them, it can happen for you, too.

So, instead of looking at someone's success as though there's a scoreboard where you're losing, start seeing it as a preview of what's coming your way. Cheer them on, genuinely. Get excited for them. Because when you do, you're shifting your energy from lack to abundance, from "Why not me?" to "I'm next." And let me tell you, when you start celebrating others, you'll be amazed at how quickly the universe starts giving you things to celebrate, too.

As I lay on the floor in my office home, wallowing in self-pity, all this was far from my mind. I wasn't in my "celebrate others era" just yet. Still, the universe was looking out for me because, at that moment, a text from Kylie popped up on my phone. She asked how I was doing and if I wanted to come visit her in Hollywood for her birthday. Girl, yes. I checked the price of a ticket. Doable.

I booked a flight right then and there. I didn't know it then, but that trip would put me on the track that would completely change my life for the better.

Kylie's birthday celebration was held at the iconic Hollywood Forever Cemetery, alongside a screening of The Addams Family. While there, she and her roommate asked if I wanted to stay and move in to their place. They didn't have a third bedroom, but they had a closet under the stairs that could "probably" fit a twin mattress. Four hundred bucks a month. Sure, why not? I got out of my office building lease, ventured back to Los Angeles, and moved into Kylie's living room closet. It wasn't even that uncomfortable.

I ended up staying in Hollywood for a few months, soaking up the sunshine, meeting new people, and remembering what it felt like to just exist without stressing over "what's next." I strolled along Santa Monica Pier, watching the street performers and eating churros, and let myself be present for the first time in what felt like forever. I spent hours on the beach, listening to the waves, feeling the warm sand between my toes, and realizing how much I had been neglecting my own happiness.

Finally, I wasn't worried about where my life was going. I wasn't obsessing over finding a partner or dating at all. I was just...living. I made new friends, laughed until my stomach hurt, attended shows, danced until sunrise at house parties in the Hollywood Hills, and let my inner child run wild. It was the kind of soul-refreshing, ego-detoxing, "remember who the heck you are" kind of experience I didn't even know I needed. I felt a newfound love and gratitude for the people in my life, and people in general, really. Most importantly, what finally clicked was that everyone is on their own journey and timeline and that their successes don't take away from my own.

My challenge to you today is to go give some praise to someone. In your real life, online, anywhere. Comment on a colleague's LinkedIn post congratulating them on their new position. Leave some love in the comment section of a blogger's recent article. Remind your sister how beautiful she is. Put that good energy everywhere.

Who and What Gets Access to You?

Fact: Your environment determines your results. So, let's make sure it's working for you, not against you. Here's a fun little exercise you can do anytime you feel you need to take inventory of the people, places, and influences around you.

Audit Your Squad

Take a hard look at who you're spending time with. Ask yourself: Do they inspire me or drain me? Do they encourage my growth or make me feel small? Are they actively building something in their life or just complaining about the same problems over and over? If someone is constantly negative, makes passive-aggressive digs at you, or downplays your ambition rather than supports it, then they do NOT get VIP access to your energy. This goes for everyone: family, close friends, acquaintances, and Chipotle employees who withhold your fair-sized blob of guac. I'm not saying cut everyone out of your life, and you don't have to make a dramatic exit. Just start spending less time engaging with people who keep you stuck and more time around people who keep you moving forward.

Surround Yourself with Expanders

Find people who are already where you want to be. Read their books. Listen to their podcasts. Join their communities. Put yourself in rooms where people with growth mindsets openly discuss investments, personal development, and success. Get around people who think making $50K a month or more is normal. Your energy will elevate to meet theirs. Likewise, if you're only around anyone who thinks small, plays small, and fears big moves, you will subconsciously adapt to their comfort zones.

Curate Your Content

Follow people on social media who expand your thinking. Unfollow accounts that make you feel behind, less than, or unworthy. It's called brain rot for a reason. Instead, fill your mind with content that supports the version of you you're building. If you spend an hour a day absorbing business tips, marketing ideas and financial advice, think about where your brain will be in six months. Now imagine if that hour were spent scrolling through chaotic drama. Only one of those pastimes leads to a glow-up.

Upgrade Your Physical Space

Having lived in an office and a closet I can attest that the rooms you spend time in matter. If your physical space is out of control with clutter, then brain fog is not a coincidence. You can't channel your inner maverick if your workspace looks chaotic. Unless, of course, you're Diane Warren. I love her, her talent, her quirks, and the amazing work she does for animals. Somehow, she can produce iconic hit records in an office piled to the ceiling with stuff! For most of us, we need a tidy environment to feel and create at our best. Declutter your space. Clear out. Your mind will feel instantly lighter.

One evening, as I lay in my under-the-stairs closet in Hollywood, scrolling through my phone, I got a message from my old Vancouver roommate and friend, Lana. "I'm newly single and moving to Toronto," she announced.

"Nice! Why Toronto?" I asked.

"Just time for a fresh start. Want to move there with me?" she asked.

I considered the idea. I'd never been to Toronto before. I looked up at the closet ceiling, or I should say, the bottom of the clothes hanging above my head. "Yeah!" I replied. And once again, Chelsea was on the move.

Last Call

On my 30th birthday, while high on Molly at a punk rock Mexican restaurant in Toronto, I decided that it was time to overhaul my life entirely. *I needed to usher in my glow-up, amigas.* Tomorrow, I would officially be "in my thirties," a certified grown-up. Thus, it was time to clean up my act and get serious about my entrepreneurial dreams. Lana and her date sat across from me at the table, listening politely as I rambled to them about how I wanted to rebrand my whole life.

At my very core, I longed to be a "real" business owner. At that stage in my life, I was still selling meme t-shirts with my dropshipping business, but it really wasn't doing much, and I didn't feel it was my *thing*. While I had just released a dream pop album for fun and was enjoying making music as a creative outlet, a life in the music industry wasn't what I wanted as a *job*.

There was something else that was meant for me; I just wasn't sure what. I had been in Toronto for a while, not really making any connections or getting anywhere. I was waitressing at a rowdy country bar, the mechanical bull kind. It was fun, sure, but again, not my *thing*.

My life choices and lack of progress were weighing on me. I had the feeling that it was time to chew off my arm to get free of them. Box up my *Coyote Ugly* era for good. What can I do to get to "The Next Step?" Whatever that means?! As we dined on burritos, I aired these grievances to my friends. My molly-pupils as big as tortillas, and hopeful for some advice.

Lana's date leaned back in the booth, sipped his drink and sighed, "Look, you already know what *isn't* working. That's half the battle." He pointed at me. "Come on. Pick a lane, test an idea, and go from there. Stop waiting for a sign. The sign is that you're already thinking about this."

Then, Lana leaned forward and looked at me thoughtfully, "I get why it feels overwhelming. You're not just looking for any business, you're looking for something that feels like your calling. And I promise, you won't find that by sitting around waiting for clarity. You'll find it by doing."

"I don't know what I'm doing or what to do," I admitted, "I want to be a business owner, but I'm just...lost."

Lana continued, "You were brave enough to pack up and move to Hollywood with no guarantees. *Twice*. Then you did it again and moved to Toronto. You produced an album from a closet. And you think you *don't* have what it takes to build something on your own?" She paused, then added, "For what it's worth, considering all the stressing and whining coming out of you, you already sound like a business owner to me."

We laughed. Maybe she was right.

As I walked to work the next morning, my pupils still gigantic from the night before (ugh), I considered what I'd been agonizing over. I think I've outgrown the life I've been living. It felt empowering to admit it. I really did want to rebrand myself and step into my full potential as an online business owner. But how? Could I make enough money online for it to be my full-time job? And I wouldn't have to bartend anymore? What about drinking? What do I do about that? Could I really be sober and still have fun in life?

These were not just big considerations; they were imperative ones. You see, I was grappling with what it means to have the *identity* of the person I wanted to become. I was struggling to reach my goals because I didn't yet believe I was the kind of person who was capable of achieving such things. I would soon learn, identity is the ultimate cheat code in life and what I was missing all along.

Identity

If you want to change your life, you can't just hope for it, wish for it, or manifest it with a cute vision board (though, let's be honest, we're still making the vision board). You have to believe that that's who you are as a person, that it's your identity. Then, you will naturally do what aligns with that identity, which ultimately leads to you goals.

This is oh-so-crucial. Taking on the identity of your best self is the first and *biggest* step in any life glow-up. For this, you basically need to update your brain's software to make it believe what your identity is now. The old version is way out of date, so it's time to delete the existing software and install a new system. How do you do this? It's actually easy. For example, if you want to quit drinking, stop saying, "I'm trying to cut back." Instead, say: "I'm not a drinker." "I don't like alcohol." That's just who you are now. There's no willpower battle every time someone offers you a cocktail because your identity doesn't even include alcohol. You're simply not that person anymore.

Say you want to be an entrepreneur. Stop telling yourself, "I aspire to be an entrepreneur." No. You're not an *aspiring* entrepreneur. You're a business owner NOW. You're a person who creates valuable products. You're someone who finds solutions, takes action, and makes things happen. Tell yourself instead, "I am an entrepreneur." Not someday. Right dang now, Susan. Quit snoozin'.

When you start seeing yourself as already being what you aspire to, your brain stops negotiating with itself. There's no internal debate about whether you should work on your business today. You're an entrepreneur, and entrepreneurs work on their businesses. There's no "Should I skip my workout today?" because you're a fit, active person, and fit, active people work out. Tell yourself that you are a best-selling author, and naturally, it's easy for you to get up early to write something every morning.

When you incorporate an identity into your being and know that is who you are, it stops being about forcing yourself to change (which feels like a chore) and starts being about living out the identity you've already claimed. And your choices become automatic rather than a struggle because they align with *who you are as a person*.

Affirm your identity, and say it out loud daily. Remember, your brain will believe you.

For a list of powerful affirmations that can help you build your identity as an entrepreneur, see the additional resources included in your bonus bundle at GlowUpYourself.com/bo nus

Identity comes first, and the results follow. This is the part people get wrong. They think they need results to prove who they are.

But no! You don't need to make six figures to call yourself an entrepreneur. You don't need to run marathons to call yourself an athlete. *You* decide who you are, and then you start acting like it. So the only question is: Who will you be now?

Take on the identity of what you *want* to be, and live in the energy of what it feels like to be that person as if your goal has already been achieved. For example, you aren't *aspiring* to be a beloved podcast host; you *are* a beloved podcast host. Embody that identity now, regardless of how many or few podcast listeners you have. You aren't "trying to be" a business owner; you are one. Know that the journey of building your business is part of the role.

When it comes to reaching goals, words like *aspiring*, *trying to*, and *becoming* and the energy around them block what we want to happen from happening. If we always think of ourselves as *aspirational*, then we are always keeping the goal out of reach. Someone who's "getting there" will never arrive at the goal. We manifest who we believe we are, remember? You aren't auditioning for a role, hoping to get picked, anymore. You're the A-lister with the leading role already. With this mindset, you will naturally do whats needed to reach your goals because it's just who you are.

Glow Up Quadrants

A few days after my 30th birthday, I moved back to Vancouver from Toronto. I was eager to figure out my new and improved healthy identity. I didn't know what my "thing," business-wise, was yet, but I had a sense that everything would work out exactly as it was supposed to. No need to rush a thing, as the universe had something up her sleeve.

First, I got my own apartment—a *real apartment*—not an office or a closet! Now, it was time to put my life rebrand desire into action. I was ready to take on the identity of the woman I dreamed of. I was ready to glow myself up, for real, this time.

I sat down to outline my master plan. Now that I had finally decided it was time to rebrand my life and meant it, I knew I couldn't just wing it. I needed a game plan. A strategy. Something to stick to that would force me to stop cycling through the same bad habits and actually embody the identity and build the life I wanted.

So, I grabbed a notebook, drew a big cross, and divided it into four sections, each one a life category for glow-up goals. I didn't have a name for this process back then, but I recently saw that TikToker Jodie Tayler (@JodieTkay) calls them "Glow-Up Quadrants," so I'll call them that moving forward.

The process of creating Glow-Up Quadrants is for activating the best version of yourself (even if, up until now, you've acted like your worst). Here are the four things I decided to focus on first:

1. **Start a business and build wealth.** I wanted financial freedom. I wanted to build something of my own. To earn an income that wasn't dependent on how generously a bar customer felt like tipping or whether an employer decided I "deserved" a raise. Plan: 1) Allocate time each day to educate myself about online businesses, passive income, and financial literacy. 2) Create a new business or offer. 3) Start keeping a budget. Put $100 into an emergency fund

each month.

2. **Upgrade my style and appearance**. I wanted to look like my new identity, the woman I now was (or would soon be), someone who is put-together, confident, and professional. And let's be real here: People treat you differently when you look like you have it together. Plan: 1) No more wearing clothes that made me feel like my past self. 2) Allocate funds to a budget and buy some new fits. 3) Study Pinterest before getting dressed each morning for inspiration.

3. **Improve my network.** We are the average of the five people we spend the most time with. Plan: 1) Take inventory of the people in my life and surround myself with positive, goal-focused individuals. 2) Nurture my healthy relationships and let the toxic ones go.

4. **Improve my health.** This was an obvious one. Plan: 1) Cut back on drinking. 2) Get more than five hours of sleep. 3)Eat more organic greens. (Could I become someone who has a morning routine?)

Instead of trying to fix everything at once, first, I gave myself four clear areas of priority, four aspects of my life that, if I focused on them, would make the biggest positive impact. I didn't want to waste time on nonessential nice-to-have changes or become overwhelmed by trying to change my entire life overnight.

Second, I created easy daily tasks or habits I could implement that would support my goals. Once I stated my goals, it was easy to see the daily actions I'd need to take to hit them out of the park. Get up earlier, work on my business aims, buy less, make more, and save more. Eat better. Drink less alcohol. I had a clear roadmap for my glow-up. I knew that if I gave myself too many tasks, I'd give up in a week. A small list felt manageable. Truly, you don't need a million goals. You just need to decide what actually matters and commit to it.

Feeling satisfied, I realized there was one more thing I wanted to do. Something I could take action on and complete right away. Whew. It was to clean up my social media and online reputation! The receipts were out there. I had spent years in the party scene, working in nightclubs, posting whatever I felt like at 2 a.m., and generally curating an online presence that was...not exactly CEO energy.

The easiest fix was to delete all my accounts and start fresh. Doing it felt so good. In a flash, my messy past was wiped clean. Heart pounding, I moved on to my phone and began deleting the numbers of anyone who was a bad influence. Not my close friends, but the sideliners. You know the ones. Delete contact. Delete contact. Delete contact.

I was officially in my rebrand era, ready to take on my new reality. Then, catching my reflection in the makeup mirror, I paused. She looked hopeful but a little unsure. *We can do this. Don't worry.* It was like a voice outside of my own. It's settled. I had made a fateful decision to reinvent myself, and I was not going to let my future self down.

Alright, so now you know what a Glow-Up Quadrant is. The only question is, what goes in yours? What four categories are most important to you at this stage in your life? Take some time to do what I did. Write down the categories and your goals for each. Then, list what you can do each day to move you closer to achieving those goals.

The Cheat Code to Achieve Any Goal

Hey, you're attempting to glow up your life while simultaneously keeping up with family, relationships, social expectations, and an inbox that just won't quit! That's wild! Seriously, who invented the idea that we're supposed to juggle business, making money, self-care, relationships, meal prepping, working out, maintaining friendships, and managing to answer texts within five business days? Well, guess what? The reality is that no one is doing it all perfectly. But if you can figure out what really matters and hone in on that, without trying to do everything, you're on the right track.

Truthfully, the secret to achieving your dream life isn't just about what you do. As I learned, it's about *who you believe you are*. Set your Glow-Up Quadrant goals based on that identity, as I did. Once you have a belief in your new identity, the next step is to give yourself "upward habits," healthy things to do that serve your identity and goals while reinforcing the truth that you are capable.

What really matters to you? To help you decide:

- What are the top 3 things that, if done consistently, will get you where you want to go?

- Which tasks are you doing just because you think you should? (Cut those.)

- What are you wasting energy on that doesn't move the needle?

Do less of the useless stuff and more of the things that make you money, bring you joy, and improve your life. Prioritize those items above all else and don't wait until you feel ready; just tackle them first. If you're waiting for the perfect moment when your life is calm, your schedule is clear, and you finally "have time" to focus on your goals, well, that moment is rare.

Maybe you said, "I want to stop overspending," or "I want to lose ten pounds." Sure, they are worthy, desired outcomes, but they feel like vague, difficult, or boring tasks. Chores! It's easy to give up on such things because you have no skin in the game.

Once again, your identity (who you believe yourself to be) will determine if you will be successful in achieving a goal. An author would write her manuscript instead of scrolling all day. A healthy person would eat clean and stretch. A YouTuber would always make time to film content. A wealthy person would prioritize smart spending and investing. Again, you don't manifest what you want. You manifest who you believe you are.

You'd be much more likely to actually reach your desired outcomes if you started believing, "I never overspend because I'm good with money," "I'm healthy, I don't like junk food," or "I'm not the kind of person who overindulges in unhealthy food." Be specific and attach your identity to your goal! That's really all there is to it.

Instead of saying things like, "I want to have a successful business," say, "I am a successful business owner, and money always flows to me." Saying, "I want to be a YouTuber," is out, and stating, "I am a YouTuber, and it's easy for me to make time to film content," is in. Notice the difference? By saying "I want to be..." you are telling yourself and the universe that you see yourself as someone who struggles with fitness, business, or confidence.

Meanwhile, recall how your brain is always working overtime to ensure it finds proof of what you tell it. That's why identity-based goals are so powerful. If you think about the last time you tried and failed to break a bad habit, chances are you were going at it by focusing on the outcome you wanted—without putting your identity in check first. Instead of focusing on outcomes, I want you to practice focusing on who you believe you are. Once you see yourself as that person, every choice becomes easier. The goals you desire turn into daily habits, and what used to feel like a chore becomes a normal and enjoyable part of your day.

TikTok creator Shelby Sacco made waves online with her easygoing rule about food. She says that she aims to eat 50–80% healthy every day. I love this approach to goals. It lets you make progress without the stress of trying to be perfect. It's refreshingly approachable. It allows for real life, like mid-day little treats, PMS cravings, and those "I'm too tired to care" pizza for dinner moments.

Here's the thing: Trying to be "100% healthy" every single day? That's a one-way ticket to burnout and bingeing on a family-sized bag of guilt. My ADHD brain refuses to follow rules or guidelines if someone else enforces them upon "us," yet it seems to love and even thrive if I'm the one making up rules. Have you experienced that yourself?

Shelby's rule is brilliant because it makes *consistency* the goal, not obsession. It says, "Hey, you're allowed to be human. You can eat a salad and also have chips and still be on track." It teaches you to trust yourself. And when you trust yourself, you *stick with it* longer. This mindset works because it focuses on momentum over rigidity. You're not punishing yourself for a "bad" meal; you're just aiming to eat the good stuff most of the time. I am so down with this concept. How about you?

Habits and Priorities

After I picked my Glow-Up Quadrants and the goals for each, based on my identity as a business owner, I then made a list of small "upward habits" to practice that would move me closer to my goal. Upward habits are things that keep you from avoiding a downward spiral. Sitting down to write your manuscript for twenty minutes every day is an upward habit. Going to the gym is an upward habit. Making time to meditate is an upward habit.

Every upward habit or action you take is a tiny vote that proves, yes, this is your new identity; you are that girl. Each time you show up, you reinforce it. The dream life glow-up isn't just about changing what you do. It's about changing *who you believe you are*. These small choices add up. And before you know it, you're not dreaming of it; you are it.

If you have ADHD, you're familiar with the random waves of hyper-focused energy that can hit you out of nowhere. Suddenly, you can tackle everything on your to-do list at superhuman speed. Dishes? Done. Emails? Answered. Business strategy? Mapped out. Closets? Organized like Marie Kondo has possessed you. But you also know what comes next: weeks of sluggish "I can't do anything" mode, where even answering a text feels like climbing Mount Everest.

Whether you have ADHD or not, waiting for the rollercoaster of focus to come around is just not sustainable when you want to glow up NOW. So, instead of relying on the arrival of wild productivity sprints, it's better to plan ahead and work in small, manageable bursts, such as:

- **Break tasks into micro steps**. Instead of deciding to "write a blog post," try "write the first paragraph." Small wins add up fast.

- **Use timers to trick your brain**, like setting a 5-minute timer. If something feels too overwhelming to start, tell yourself you'll do it for just five minutes. Too busy to work on your business? Spend five minutes sending one email. Can't commit to a full workout? Stretch for five minutes. Feeling behind on content creation? Write one idea down. Half the battle is just getting started. Then, nine times out of ten, once you start, you keep going.

- **Ride the motivation wave when it hits**, but don't expect it to last forever. Think of it like it's a Wi-Fi signal; the signal may come and go, so download as much progress as you can while it's strong, but remember to pace yourself, too.

Remember, even the biggest trees started as tiny seeds. It's all about creating high-impact actions and habits that move the needle in your life and business without burning yourself out, ghosting your friends, or losing your mind in the process.

Another one of one of my favorite tactics is *habit stacking*. Habit stacking is a term coined by James Clear in his book, *Atomic Habits*, and is the simple practice of combining multiple habits at once. For example, I want to exercise every day, and I also want to tackle all the books I've been meaning to read. So, I habit stack walking on the treadmill under my standing desk while I write a blog post, so I pair exercise with my writing work. It's recommended that you stack habits by pairing them with other habits that you already have. This creates a routine that makes it easier to stick to your habits.

Habit stacking is also a good way to encourage new habits by attaching them to the ones you already do. For example, if you want to get into the habit of journaling every morning, do it while your coffee is brewing. Trying to read more? Keep a book in the bathroom (let's be real, we all scroll there anyway). Can you do squats while brushing your teeth? Love that for you. If you've ever forgotten to take your vitamins, drink enough water, or respond to a text before it became a historical artifact, you need habit stacking. You're already doing stuff every day; just attach new habits to existing ones and watch your consistency skyrocket.

Finally, please, please stop letting other people's priorities dictate your schedule. Of course, if you have kids, they are high up there in your priorities. Yet, you are not obligated to be available 24/7 to coworkers, relatives, neighbors, friends, or telemarketers. You can say no, and the world will not implode. If you're constantly saying yes to things you don't want to do just to keep the peace, guess what? You're draining the energy you need to build your dream life.

On that note, you've probably compared where you are in business to where another entrepreneur is in his, and you've felt behind. You know, the gurus on social media who attribute their success to their hustle-focused morning routine. They wake up before sunrise to meditate in a silent home. Then, they read three chapters of a self-development book before grinding for six hours uninterrupted.

Let's consider the possibility that many of these successful men have built-in life managers (AKA wives) handling everything for them. Many even have wives who cook, clean, and manage their lives entirely, allowing them to remain in the creative flow with ease. Can you imagine? They aren't pausing their workflow every five minutes to make a snack for their kid or defuse a toddler meltdown. They're not worrying about laundry, meal planning, doctors' appointments, or home management.

Meanwhile, you're trying to build your empire while juggling fifty-seven other responsibilities. You're trying to gather your thoughts so you can record a webinar *for one dang hou*r without a child bursting into the room, screaming at you.

So, know that you are not failing because your business isn't scaling at record speed. You're not less capable. You simply have a completely different reality than the guy telling you to "just hustle harder." That advice is not applicable to you. And that's okay. *Stop measuring yourself against people who don't even do their own laundry!*

In all honesty, your success will take longer, and that does not mean it's less valid. You're doing something even more badass: you're building a business amid total chaos. At day's end, congratulate yourself on what you do get done, no matter how much or how little. If you sent one important email, that's a win. If you took one step toward your goals, that's progress! If you made one small healthy choice, go you! Let's stop beating ourselves up for not doing everything perfectly and start celebrating what we are doing just fine.

When you break up with your old self and outdated mindset you create space for the new and improved version of you to operate. Delete the unhelpful stories playing on repeat in that beautiful brain of yours. Rewire. Reclaim. Reinstall a mindset that's compatible with your purpose. And while we're at it, you might need to lovingly unsubscribe from some people, too. Now, let's talk about your business.

5

Building a Business that Elevates Your Lifestyle

If you're reading this book, you're ready to elevate your life, improve your financial future, and step into the role of your most successful self. Turning some of your skills into a business is a natural step. This means it's time to stop treating your business like a hobby and start taking it seriously.

Here's the reality, chicky. You don't need some big epiphany before you take action. Just dream up the lifestyle you wish to have, and then start. Build skills, try things, fail at things, learn from things. Repeat. What's something you enjoy? What's a skill you can monetize? What excites you? What do people already come to you for advice about? What would you be happy doing even if it didn't pay anything at first?

As I mentioned previously, it doesn't have to be a grand passion. The best indicator of what you should monetize is what gives you a spark of excitement. Following that spark can lead you to make a living doing something you enjoy. But that doesn't mean you should monetize every single one of your passions or that everything you enjoy should become a business. Just because you are passionate about something doesn't mean someone else will pay for it.

How do you know which passions to monetize and which to leave as hobbies? Well, that all comes down to the lifestyle you want to have. Here's how to look at whether something is a potential business or should stay a hobby.

A Hobby = Something You Enjoy, With Zero Pressure to Perform

A hobby is a passion that you don't need to bring in any money because it provides you with joy in its purest form. It's gardening with zero plans to sell a single cucumber. It's rollerskating in an '80s leotard. No deadlines, no pressure. (Well, some of us would feel pressure wearing a leotard in public, but that's beside the point). Can you make money from it? Maybe, but you don't have to. Would it ruin the fun if you tried to monetize it? Probably. Keep your hobbies. Everyone needs things in life that are just for enjoyment.

A Business = Something That Solves a Problem and Makes You Money.

This is where your passion meets money. It's something you enjoy doing and would enjoy getting paid to do. The key here is that it solves a problem (big or small) for other people and that they'll pay you for it, whether directly (client work) or indirectly (ad revenue, affiliate sales, or brand deals).

What kind of problem-solving will people pay for? A big problem people have is doing their taxes correctly. You could charge clients to do their bookkeeping and file their taxes. A small problem people have is boredom. You can entertain them with your blog or social media content, and when they watch, you earn money indirectly through ad networks for those views. Both are businesses.

So, ask yourself, what am I actually doing? If you love an activity but would rather keep it sacred and stress-free, it's a hobby. Protect it. If you're solving problems people should or will pay for, it's a business. Run it like one.

In a nutshell, a hobby is a passion you love with zero pressure to perform. A business is a passion that solves someone's problem and makes you money. The key is to monetize one of your passions and make it a business.

Know that you don't have to do this alone. Build a network, even if it's just online. Start talking about your ideas, even before they feel fully formed. The more you put yourself out there, the more opportunities will find you. Like I said before, successful people don't wait for the perfect idea; they just start. Because it's simply a part of the inner workings of the lifestyle they are set on having. Let's be more like that.

Good Vibes

Someone on TikTok said, "The secret to happiness is being obsessed with yourself and being kind to others." It's so true. To start embodying the frequency of the woman you envision you are becoming, allow yourself to become obsessed with yourself, believe in your goals, and be kind and loving to everyone. Then, watch the magic unfold. And I do mean be kind to everyone. For example, if you don't already do this, catch spiders to free them outside instead of killing them. When you do, take a moment to really feel how good it feels to choose compassion. The universe rewards those who are kind, especially when it's kindness to those who can do nothing for you.

The morning after I'd created my first Glow-Up Quadrants goals, I woke up feeling a new sense of capability. Like I could do anything, and I hadn't even done anything yet. The feeling of setting goals was exciting. I wanted to take action on my new life plans right away so I could relish what it would feel like to accomplish them.

From that moment on, I felt an overwhelming confidence that embodied a feeling of yes, I'm on the right track. I started becoming more aware of my spending, so saving became easier. It became a normal part of my day to look for ways to make more money. I ramped up my online pursuits, and I started taking part-time cleaning jobs for extra cash.

Then I started "drop servicing," where I'd sell a digital media service to business owners who would have people on gig sites perform jobs. At this time, I stopped working in night clubs and instead started bartending at a live music venue, the Rickshaw, which was a much healthier work environment. Working there just three nights a week meant that I had lots of free time to create, write, and take care of myself. A luxury.

The light bulb moment came when I realized that all the tech/website building stuff I'm really good at was a skill that a lot of people didn't have but needed. What was so easy for me, like building websites and content marketing, was hard for others. I'd been building websites for local businesses for a few years, here and there. So, I began offering website-building services online to small business owners worldwide. This is where I really thrived. Working on websites and blogging was something I enjoyed. I learned soon enough that whatever it is you enjoy is your magic. Follow that enjoyment, follow the excitement. That is the thing to monetize.

In just a few months, I had grown my savings. I was in the green! It wasn't a huge number yet, but seeing that number in my bank account made me glow. It was the first time I started feeling like someone who was capable of becoming rich. I was simply vibrating at a higher level because I had taken the time to consider what I really wanted my life to be like, mapped out my goals, and then stuck to the plan.

Most importantly, I believed in and acted like my goals were already achieved. I took on the identity of someone who's good with money by frequently saying out loud, "I'm good with money!" and before long, I was seeing proof that it was true. I didn't know exactly what manifesting was back then, but I was practicing it nonetheless.

I looked healthier, too. Though not yet fully sober yet, I'd majorly cut back on drinking and eliminated all spirits in favor of wine. Baby steps are still steps. And, obviously, no more molly. My savings continued to grow, and pretty soon, I had saved enough for a down payment. Becoming a homeowner was now a possibility, not just a wish!

Then I met him. I spotted him across the crowded bar. Oh, there he is, the words floated across my mind. It was just so obvious, like I'd known him forever. It was as if it was all planned out for us all along, and our Spirit Guides were just standing by their screens screaming because this was the season finale they'd been eagerly planning out, scripting, arranging, just waiting for us to perform. "Here they go! Don't mess this up, little ones!" they probably squealed as Nick and I introduced ourselves on the dance floor.

The connection was instant, electric. Around him, I felt calm, present, and at home. Naturally, we eloped three weeks later, running off to Vegas and getting matching "Till Death" tattoos. Yep, that happened. You might think deciding to marry someone after knowing them for only three weeks is fast, but actually, we decided to put a ring on it three days after meeting.

Our wedding was in old Vegas at an Elvis chapel. The officiant, an Elvis impersonator in a full white jumpsuit with a cape, cracked jokes and sang as he officiated, "Fear of commitment has left the building." We didn't tell anyone beforehand because we knew our friends and family would scrutinize how fast we were moving and try to stop us. But we just knew it was right. Although the surprise nuptials were a shock to Nick's and my family and friends at first, we are still going strong a decade later.

Finding a partner and getting married wasn't one of my Glow-Up Quadrants. That said, it turned out to be a welcome perk of stepping up to the altar of change.

When I wasn't looking, when I had finally learned to love my own company, when I had stopped chasing and just started being, that's when I met my husband. Oh, the irony! Not when I was desperately trying to control everything but when I was busy loving myself. Turns out, "missing pieces" have a way of finding you when you're already whole. That's cheesy. Thank you. Thank you very much.

Portals

It was the spring of 2016. I was in Hawaii with Nick, sitting by the hotel pool. I'd been feeling weird for a few days. I didn't feel like taking advantage of the pool bar menu. I was lethargic and acting kind of bitchy, but I wasn't sure why. A queasy, sluggish, seasick feeling had been lingering for days. Nick wanted to go sightseeing, swimming, and dining.

Ugh, I should be enjoying the warm weather and acting more fun, but I just felt gross. Did I eat something bad? No, I didn't have a stomach ache, so it probably wasn't food poisoning. Am I hungover? No. What the heck?!

Oh. Perhaps I should take a pregnancy test. Of course! I bet that's what this is. Nick and I made our way to the nearest CVS and bought a box of two little pregnancy test sticks. He was giddy that this might be happening. I, on the other hand, felt terrified that I might be pregnant and that it would end in another miscarriage.

The previous fall, we had discovered we were expecting, only to find out we were no longer expecting. Memories flashed in my mind's eye, first of writhing in unbearable pain then of the deep sadness that kept me in bed for days long after the physical pain subsided.

Ugh, snap out of it, Chelsea! You are in Hawaii! You have a freaking flower tucked behind your ear! You have adorable Betty bangs and a puka shell necklace! PUKA SHELL.

We went to a classy, aesthetic sushi restaurant for dinner. I peed on the stick in the restaurant's bathroom. After tossing the pee stick in my purse, I slid back to our table. I waited for the blue line to appear or not, for what felt like an eternity. "Is it time yet?" Nick asked again. We ordered some appetizers. "How about now?"

Always a class act, I pulled the pee stick out of my bag and held it up to the candle at our table. No dice. "I'm not knocked up," I announced. "Oh, too bad," he sighed affectionately.

The result was fine. But for Nick's sake, I felt really guilty about my sluggishness the past few days. I wasn't being the fun, bubbly travel companion he'd probably been imagining as we flew in for this trip. And to top it off, I wasn't pregnant, so I didn't have that good news as an excuse for my sluggish mood, either.

Also, I wished I had an appetite to eat. The menu looked amazing, but with the queasiness, I just couldn't do it. I played with the straw in my ginger ale and wondered, If not preggo, then what's this feeling?

A few days later, we were back home in Vancouver, unpacking our suitcases. I found the pregnancy test box with the second stick still inside. The sluggish, seasick feeling still hadn't gone away, so

I decided to check again. This time, the results were conclusive. I was pregnant. Cool!

With this news, avoiding alcohol was a no-brainer. Because, obviously, you don't drink when you're pregnant. I had the ultimate excuse to refuse drinks now, and no one could guilt-trip me about it. It was like stepping into a portal, into a totally new life where sobriety was just normal. Finally.

At that time in my life, I was working two jobs. I worked as a marketing manager at the business brokerage on weekdays from 9 a.m. to 4 p.m. Then, I was still bartending at the Rickshaw three nights a week from 6 p.m. to 1 a.m. Thursdays and Fridays were the most intense because I had just a short time to walk from my office in Coal Harbour to the East Side, where the Rickshaw was located, for my night job. At least it was summertime, so the fresh air was nice.

Working at the Rickshaw while pregnant was actually a lot of fun. I'd wear tight-fitting bodycon dresses as my belly and cleavage grew massive, and my tips had never been so good. Maybe people were into a baddie pregnant chick making their drink. Or maybe they felt bad that this poor pregnant mother was "stuck" slinging drinks at a noisy venue. Either way, fine by me. They tipped well. *Cha-ching!*

Although, as the months went on, it became more strenuous to work the job. I told my boss at the Rickshaw right away that I was pregnant before I started showing. I didn't want to hide it from him; I wanted to keep him in the loop. He was super accommodating when I needed to abandon the bar a couple of times a night for more frequent pee breaks, thanks to pregnancy bladder.

Once it became hard to stand for seven hours, he ensured there was always a bucket behind the bar for me to sit on when needed. The other bartenders and staff were also super sweet, not letting me carry any ice buckets or anything too heavy. I will remember their kindness forever.

My office job, however, was another situation. I chose to keep my pregnancy secret from everyone there. Because I was a new hire and still in my probationary period, I didn't want to risk getting canned. Hiding my pregnancy at the office job was fairly easy for the first few months. I would wear long scarves every day to cover my growing belly and would keep to myself as much as possible.

On my first day working there, I took note of every one of my new coworkers' names and immediately blocked them all on all social media. This was so I could I keep a low profile and keep my office life completely separate from my personal life. Also, so no one could discover my pregnancy online. But by the time I was nearing my third trimester, my tummy was becoming harder to hide.

One time, as I reached for something in the break room in front of a coworker, my shirt rose up, and my scarf slipped. I quickly adjusted them, but it was too late. The look on my coworker's face was obvious. Oh my god, she noticed my baby belly. She knew! Yet, she said nothing. Love her for that.

Around this time, Nick and I were approved for a mortgage. We bought an apartment in Victoria on Vancouver Island. It was a one-bedroom in an old 1970s building with popcorn ceilings, rundown appliances, and some carpets that have seen better days. We loved it and were so excited to finally be homeowners, ready to start our first renovation project together. In the first few months of my pregnancy, we took the ferry to Victoria on some weekends to work on the apartment. Nick would rip things out while I painted. We slept on a mattress on the living room floor and then ferried back to Vancouver on Sunday night. I was absolutely living my HGTV dreams. I was so happy.

Finally, by my eighth-month pregnancy milestone, I'd been at the job 600 hours. This meant I had banked up enough hours to be eligible for my maternity leave. (In Canada, you need to work 600 consecutive hours at a job to access your government-arranged maternity leave money that you've been paying into since your first job.) I will never forget how good it felt to hand in my resignation! FREEDOM! The feeling of quitting felt oh-so-good. My desk chair was left spinning 100 miles a minute as I jumped out of it and ran out of that building so fast. Or, as fast as I could waddle.

That day, as I left the lobby and stepped onto the street, I promised myself I would never work another office or bar job again. I'm still keeping that promise to myself today. It was time to rest and get ready to lay this giant egg. It was funny. As soon as I stopped working, my body went, "OK, we can finally stop hiding! Let's balloon!" I morphed into my full preggo form and just took it easy as I awaited the big day.

I gave birth to our son right before Christmas Eve in 2016. It was a C-section, so I had to stay in the hospital for four days after the birth. During those four days, Nick moved all of our belongings from our rental apartment in Vancouver to our new apartment in Victoria.

As soon as the hospital released me and the baby, we headed straight to the ferry to start our new life on Vancouver Island. I had booked a basement suite on Airbnb for us to stay in for the first few days while Nick got the apartment set up. After all, we hadn't set up a bed or unpacked any boxes yet.

When we pulled up to the Airbnb, the hosts who lived upstairs greeted us in the driveway. "Oh, that's a tiny baby!" the woman said, surprised at the newborn. "When was this little guy born?"

"On Wednesday," I shrugged. Probably too casually. I don't know. Everything was a blur. In those first hazy weeks of motherhood, I was sleep-deprived and overwhelmed, trying to process the staggering reality that my life had changed forever. Days blurred into nights, and even basic hygiene felt like an Olympic sport. I existed in a strange, foggy postpartum cloud. I'd reach into the fridge to get something and then immediately forget what I needed. Hmm...I really hope I put the almond milk, not breast milk, in this coffee.

Some nights, I'd wake up in a panic from crazy, anxiety-ridden nightmares, scenes where I'd lost my kid. Other nights, I wouldn't have the chance to dream, as Nick and I would be up rocking our newborn night owl baby who refused to sleep.

I'm a mom now. I am responsible for someone other than myself, I thought, as I bagged up all my pleather bodycon dresses and platform heels for the donation bin. Quite literally shipping my party girl past away. The words felt surreal, like trying on a new identity that didn't quite fit yet. Everything had shifted, and there was no going back to my old life. One thing was crystal clear: I simply HAD to follow through with my dreams of being an entrepreneur now.

If I thought I had time to fiddle around and procrastinate on my goals before, I certainly didn't have time now. Becoming a mom flipped a switch in me. It wasn't just about myself anymore. This time I had a real reason to give it my all. I had to focus on creating a life that would give my child security, freedom, and a future where he'd never have to struggle the way I did. There were no two ways about it; now I was determined.

Virtual Reality

It was 3 a.m., in February 2017. I was sitting up in bed, feeding my newborn. Instead of feeling all sorts of new mom bliss they say you're supposed to experience, I was feeling all sorts of worries about our future. I needed to find a way to make money and felt desperate to figure something out.

The thought of having to put my tiny son in daycare to return to the workforce felt wrong. But what else was there to do? My maternity leave and its small pay were going to run out eventually. That night, as I held him in my arms, I looked up at the ceiling and silently made a wish, asking for someone to help guide me.

The next morning, I was scrolling through social media when something caught my eye. Something that shook me out of my postpartum haze and would change my life forever. There, in my feed, was an ad for a virtual business summit about course creators. I didn't know what a virtual summit was then, but tickets were free, and I could watch it from home, so I reasoned, why not? Maybe I'd learn something. Maybe it would be background noise while I figured out how to be a mom.

I signed up to watch the summit, not expecting anything. Let me tell you, whoever was listening to my "ask" the night before got the message and delivered help to me fast. At that moment, I had no idea that clicking that ad would change my life.

It was a five-day virtual summit. I watched every single session, live, from my couch. Each day I grew more and more excited. I listened as bloggers, digital product sellers, and course creators shared their startup stories. These are real people who built digital businesses and made money online. And that's when it clicked: This wasn't just something "other people" were doing. It wasn't a scam or something only celebrities could do. It was happening. It was possible. If they could do it, why couldn't I?

That very day, I launched a cruelty-free beauty blog. It was a place to celebrate brands that did not test their products on animals or use animal-derived ingredients. I'm an animal lover, a vegetarian, and an advocate for keeping animals out of cosmetics testing, so it felt right. I didn't have a business plan, but I had a mission to create content that brought attention to ethical brands in the beauty industry. That was enough to keep me interested.

While I had dabbled in blogging before, let's be honest, it was a glorified hobby then. This time, it was going to be a business. Every day, while my newborn slept or nursed, I wrote. For hours. It was not glamorous. Sometimes, I questioned my sanity. Yet I had this feeling, deep in my gut, that this was my shot if only I could just hold on and get the next post up...

I read all the blog income reports I could find on the Internet and gleaned that for a brand-new blog, the money was in affiliate marketing, meaning promoting products through brand-partner links in your blog. So, I monetized my site immediately with affiliate links. Back then, it felt like the easiest entry point to making money. I recommended products I used and loved, and poured my heart into writing product reviews. When I got my first affiliate commission, I was elated! $65.10! I wanted to cry; I was so happy. It was proof that the thing I was building was actually working.

Next, I created a digital product (a cruelty-free beauty tips PDF) and used it as a lead magnet to grow a newsletter around my blog. I focused on email marketing as a way to grow a community, and posted my article links to Pinterest for traffic growth. Before I knew it, people were reading my blog posts! They were signing up for my newsletter and were buying the affiliate products I recommended! With each commission notification, I'd get another dopamine hit. This was AWESOME.

I quickly became addicted (in the best kind of way) to my healthy new obsession, blogging. When my traffic reached 25,000 sessions, I was accepted into an ad network, which meant advertisers would pay to place ads on my site. Suddenly, my little blog was producing $1,200 a month in income as I worked from home, from my couch, while I held my baby. And let me tell you, seeing that first ad revenue payment hit my account for the first time was a MOMENT.

Naturally, because I can't sit still when I see an opportunity, I started a second website, HerPaperRoute.com. With this website, I focused on documenting my journey in the creator economy.

I shared everything I was learning about blogging, affiliate marketing, and digital products. I was determined to work so hard online that I wouldn't have to return to the workforce once my maternity leave ran out. (In Canada paid maternity leave is a year). And I hoped that my transparency about what I was learning in my posts on HerPaperRoute would help someone else on their money journey.

If you're wondering where the name HerPaperRoute came from, it's a simple play on words. "Her" is you, "paper" refers to money, and "route" is your path to get that money!

Then, because I was still riding the high from that summit, I decided to launch a course. I didn't know what I was doing, but I thought, If the speakers at the summit can do it, I can too. So, I made a course on dropshipping since that was what I knew best at the time. As it turned out, knowing the strategies for how to sell as a dropshipper did not mean teaching them came easily.

In fact, recording my first course was a disaster. I faced a major learning curve with it. I didn't have a fancy aesthetic office or even a tidy corner to serve as the backdrop for recording the lessons. My apartment was under renovation. Nick's tools and materials were everywhere, along with half-finished projects. What's worse, I couldn't get through a single take without forgetting what I was saying. As soon as I hit record, my brain would short-circuit. Oh, I suddenly developed a stuttering speech impairment, cool.

And then there was my baby. He wasn't on board with this whole "Mom needs silence to record" plan. He fussed, he cried, and he made random baby noises that definitely weren't helping me sound like a professional educator. I tried waiting for a quiet moment. There weren't any.

So, I did what every mom eventually learns to do. I adapted. I picked him up. I held him in my arms while I recorded the lessons. So that's how my students got their course from me. I explained strategies while holding a newborn. And you know what? They loved it. I got messages from students that said, "That was the most relatable thing ever." Yep. This is real life. This is what bootstrapping looks like. No fancy studio. No team. No polished perfection. Just a mom, a laptop, and an unshakable belief that this was going to work.

I'm sharing this with you because I know how hard it is to start. I know how overwhelming it feels when you're juggling a million things, when you're doubting yourself, and when you don't have a single "quiet" moment to work.

I know the mental gymnastics of wondering if this is even possible for you. And I'm here to tell you: It is. Start messy. Start before you feel ready.

Remember, every single person you see making money online had to start somewhere. I started on my couch, holding a baby, in a messy apartment in mid-renovation. You can start exactly where you are.

What You Should Sell: Workshop Exercise

Obviously, if you want to make money online, you need something to sell. Period. End of story. Let's figure out something you can sell.

Think about what you're already good at because that is your starting point. Are you great at writing? Freelance. Good at organizing? Offer digital planners. Obsessed with social media? Manage accounts for small businesses drowning in DMs. The fastest way to start making money is to monetize a skill you already have instead of waiting until you've "learned enough" about something else. You are already qualified to help someone with something. Slap a price tag on it, girl!

It doesn't matter how pretty your font is, how many TikTok followers you have, or how many money mindset affirmations you sing to your cat. You do not have a business if you do not have an offer. And yet, this is where so many people get stuck. They overthink. They wait for the "perfect" idea. They procrastinate like it's a bottomless procrastination brunch. No more. We are figuring this out today.

But what's that? Oh, I already know what's happening right now. Your mind is racing, coming up with every possible reason as to why you shouldn't start.

- But what if my idea is no good?
- But what if I get sick of this niche after I launch?

- But what if no one buys it?
- But what if I secretly hate running a business?
- But what if an asteroid hits Earth, and none of this even matters?

And while I respect your ability to create elaborate, dramatic roadblocks out of thin air (it's very creative, honestly), I will need you to STOP. RIGHT. THERE.

This is just ONE offer. You do not have to commit to this idea forever. You do not have to make your entire brand about it. You do not have to sign a blood oath saying this is your life's work.

We are taking action on ONE offer to get it out of your head and into the real world, where it can actually make you money. Because right now, you're making it way harder than it needs to be. Your idea is bouncing around in your brain, spiraling into a tornado of overthinking. When really, it should be focused on your sales page, taking payments. It's that simple. Not perfecting and not waiting until you feel ready. Not agonizing over whether it's The One.

Just launch something and prove to yourself how easy it actually is to get a digital product to market. So let's cut the excuses and get this thing live, OK, babe? Grab a notebook, and let's run this exercise to figure out your offer idea right here and now.

Step 1. List 10 things you're good at (yes, you are good at things). If your brain just screamed, "But I don't have any skills!" shut that down immediately. You are alive, functioning, and have made it this far. You have skills. Write down everything you know how to do, no matter how random. Things people ask for your help with. Things you enjoy doing. Things you've learned from past jobs, hobbies, or life experiences.

Step 2. Now list 10 problems you can solve. Business is not about you. It's about solving a problem for someone else. People pay for solutions. So now, look at your list from Step 1 and ask, How can this help someone else? What problem does this skill or knowledge solve? Who would pay for this? As an example, suppose you're terrific at meal prepping.

The problem you solve: Busy people don't have time to cook and eat like garbage because of it.

Potential offer: Meal prep plans, grocery lists, and done-for-you weekly menus.

Here's another example. I'm really good at shrinking nice wool sweaters in the washing machine. I ruin my expensive clothes all the time this way. Is this a service I could sell? At first thought, probably not, unless people buy sweaters that are too big for them. But I'm not going to shut down this skill! Why? Because in this exercise, we are coming up with product ideas for *every* skill, regardless of how niche or seemingly useless. Let's focus on the problem. Shrinking nice clothes is a problem people have. Forgetting that your expensive dry-clean-only sweater got mixed up with the rest of the laundry is a problem.

What are some business ideas we could think up to solve this problem? How about smart laundry tags for certain types of clothing that aggressively beep an alarm at you if you try to wash them? You could scan your laundry basket with your phone, and an app will tell you, "SOS, there's a dry-clean-only item in here." Or how about a smart-lock washer and dryer that won't start a cycle if it detects any wool items inside?

Here are some more examples to get your brain moving:

- Are you obsessed with budgeting and saving money? Teach it. Sell budget templates. Start a finance blog.

- Good at Canva? Offer Instagram templates for business owners.

- Know your way around a garden? Sell a "Grow Your First Veggie Garden" guide.

- Have experience freelancing? Sell a pitch template pack for new freelancers.

- Love fashion? Sell personal styling guides or wardrobe checklists.

- Are you great at organizing? People pay for decluttering help, digital planners, and home organization courses.

- Tech-savvy? Businesses need help setting up websites, automation, and workflows.

Let's keep going. Pick one as your first offer. *Yes, right now!* Simply look at your list and pick ONE thing. Not the "perfect" idea. Not the one that "feels safe." Just any one. If you had to make an offer today, what is it? A service? A product? A course? A digital download? No more overthinking. Make a decision. You can always refine it later.

Congratulations, you now have your offer idea! If you're still unsure, know that this exercise helps you find what you enjoy and what you're good at. The point of it is to get you into the habit of thinking like an entrepreneur, which is being able to figure out how your knowledge could be packaged to help someone else. And to uncover what feels fun. I just want to reiterate this point: This offer doesn't have to be perfect or even close to it. It simply has to exist.

Bootstrapping Your Business

Starting a business doesn't have to mean draining your savings or selling a kidney to buy a ring light. Bootstrapping is the name of the game. It's when you build something yourself. No investors, no team. Just you in the driver's seat, creatively and financially. Your vision. Your pace. Your way.

It's how I built HerPaperRoute back then, and it's how I still build new brands today. I didn't start my business from a perfect home office, have any fancy equipment, or any real business plan. I started it from my couch, recovering from a C-section, half-delirious from sleep deprivation, holding a newborn. It all started because I clicked on an ad, trusted my intuition, and just followed a spark of excitement to see where it might lead.

So, how do one bootstrap their new business idea to get it off the ground? First, use what you already have. You don't need high-end software or a massive marketing budget to start. Use free tools like Canva for design, a low-cost or free email service provider for email marketing, and Google Docs for as much as you can.

Anytime you sit down to work, ask, "Could AI assist me in this task somehow?" the answer is usually yes. Explore free AI tools that can make your workload easier. Leverage what you have before investing in expensive extras.

Next, you're going to build an online presence, either for free or as low cost as needed. You don't need a perfect website on day one (or ever, honestly). Launch with social media and a simple one-page website. Pinterest, TikTok, and Instagram are free tools at your fingertips for marketing, brand awareness, and sales. Just consistently show up online and talk about what you do. The more people see you, the more they trust you, and the more they'll want to buy from you.

Hot tip: the fastest way to start making money is to monetize a skill you already have instead of waiting until you've "learned enough" about something else. You are already qualified to help someone with something. Slap a price tag on it, girl!

Finally, spend a bit of time each day networking. No, you don't have to cold DM strangers with "Hey, boss babe!" messages. You don't have to show up at seminars wearing an ill-fitting power suit, either. Instead, genuinely engage online with people in your industry. Comment on posts, join online communities, and collaborate with others. Opportunities come from connections, and building relationships doesn't cost a dime.

If I can encourage you to embrace the DIY phase, then we're on the right track here. Because at first, you'll be wearing all the hats: CEO, marketing team, customer service rep, and probably your own intern. It's messy, but it's worthwhile. This phase teaches you how to run a lean, profitable business instead of throwing money at every shiny new tool.

You're learning high-income skills every day now, and through this trial and error, you are going to discover talents you never knew existed. You'll also discover that you absolutely hate some tasks, which is great! Knowing this now means you'll know exactly what tasks to outsource later. The more you DIY in the beginning, the better you'll understand what's worth outsourcing later, which will make the process of hiring easier.

So, I'd encourage any new business owner to look at bootstrapping as a valuable on-the-job training ground. It's never a waste of time if you are enjoying the process of up-leveling your skills. Just one more accolade to add to your glow-up!

Lean Into It

In the beginning, think *lean*. Don't make the mistake of assuming you have to think big when starting a new business venture. This is especially true if you struggle with procrastination and getting going. What is the easiest, fastest, most cost-effective way to get the offer from the previous section up for sale? Now, challenge yourself to do it so it's up for sale *today*!

Really! Not only is this a good practice for getting into the habit of taking action on ideas fast, but as women with kids, ADHD, or both—it's essential. The quicker you move from idea to action, the less time that idea has to get buried under your to-do list.

Like everything, ideas are energy. When you get an idea for a new video, hit record and put that idea out into the world now. Don't wait until tomorrow when your makeup's on or you've tidied your room. Your performance will be 100% better when the idea is fresh. Viewers can sense that excited energy through the camera. I believe that ideas can flow from person to person, too. Meaning, if you don't take action on an idea, it will move on to someone who will.

Michael Jackson was a pro at acting on his ideas immediately, whether it was a new song or the stage design for his tour. He knew that waiting could mean the idea could flow to someone else and even said, "If I don't act on my ideas, God will give them to Prince!" Think about how many times you have had an idea but didn't pursue it. Then, you see someone else making your idea a reality. It's frustrating, right?

Lean also means stop thinking you have to throw money at your idea. I bet you think starting a business means draining your savings for a logo or that you need to pay a coach to help you make money. Truthfully, that's all nonsense. Do you know what you *actually* need? A product or service someone is willing to pay for. That's it. The rest is just extra.

Here's a list of things you absolutely *don't need* so you can stop stressing about them.

- **A website on day one**. Although I fully believe that

every creator should have a website, you can sell through social media, email, or a free landing page. Your website can come later when you have actual customers.

- **A business plan that's longer than one page**. Unless you're planning on pitching to investors (unlikely), you don't need a 50-page document collecting dust on your Google Drive. A simple one-pager with your idea, audience, and pricing is plenty. You are probably the only person who will read it, so make it enough to organize your ideas and save the lengthy explanations.

- **A tagline?** Cute but unnecessary. A "company values" chart? You can figure that out after you have made money.

- **Fancy branding**. A Canva logo and some free fonts will get you further than you think. Don't waste months agonizing over colors.

- **Advertising**. Do you really need to drop a bunch of cash on ads? Probably not in the beginning. And certainly not until you've seen conversions (sales) on your offer occur organically.

- **A business loan or investors.** Bootstrapping forces you to be creative and test ideas cheaply. You don't need debt! Just resourcefulness. Plus, expenses will be minimal if you are starting a digital business.

Now, here's a list of what you *actually need*.

- **An offer**. What are you selling, and how does it help people? The first versions won't be perfect, and that's okay. You'll tweak it as you go. Sell first, refine later. We will go over how to create your offer in a moment.

- **An audience**. Whether it's on Instagram or TikTok, to your email list, or just to a group text with five people, right now, start talking about what you're doing. If no one knows you have an offer, no one can buy it.

- **A way to collect money**. PayPal, Stripe, Venmo, whatever. (More on this in the next section.) Just make it easy.

- **Consistent Action**. It won't be perfect. You'll cringe at your early work. Post it anyway.

- **Resilience**. The first time someone ghosts you or asks for a refund, don't spiral. Adjust and keep going.

Once you have an idea for an offer, know that you need to act on it, quick. Yo*ur new rule is to sell first and perfect your offer later*. Let it go. Your customers don't care about the fluff. They care about what you're selling and how it helps them. So instead of staring at a blank Google Doc, obsessing over your "brand essence," go sell something today. Even if it's messy. Even if it's not perfect. Even if it's just a simple Instagram post saying, "Hey, I'm offering this thing. Want in?" You don't need the prettiest website. Just get out there and start selling. And for the love of all things holy, do not spend another minute agonizing over your tagline. It's time to make some money. Who's ready to create an offer?

How to Create an Offer, Step by Step

So, you've selected one idea, are ready to monetize it, and have expanded your online presence. Great! Here's my advice for the quickest, most efficient way to get your offer up for sale. If you follow this process, there should be no reason why you can't have it available for purchase within three hours from now. For this exercise, I'll be using an ebook as an example.

Start by going to Pinterest Trends or Google Trends and spend ten minutes searching for trends related to your offer. If my offer is about meal planning, I'd check the food category. I'd search for trends linked to keywords like "meal planning," "quick meals,"and "easy prep meals." Then, I'd see what issues people face with meal planning. I'd use that info to shape my offer.

If your audience is busy parents, maybe a problem they have is coming up with easy kids' lunches to pack for school. You could create a 30-day meal plan for healthy school lunches that takes the guesswork out for parents. Your offer could be an ebook that includes grocery lists and a process for packing and freezing a week of lunches so parents get their mornings back.

Pop over to Canva to create your ebook for free. It's very easy. Don't try to fill it with unnecessary fluff; just give them the goods. Your ebook should only be as long as needed to get the solution sorted for your customer. Don't worry if design isn't your wheelhouse either; Canva has many great templates. You can also use

Canva templates to create mockups of your ebook and graphics for social media. Export it as a PDF, and *voilà*, your digital product is done. Seriously, it's easy nowadays to launch products thanks to tools like this.

The next thing you'll need is some sort of payment processor, which is just a fancy term for an online system that facilitates people giving you money. You know, the modern-day equivalent of a cash register, but without needing a drawer full of pennies. This way, people can throw their money at you instead of just "liking" your content and moving on.

There are many options. The one you choose must:

- 1) allow someone to enter their credit card info
- and 2) send the customer your digital product automatically. You know, so you don't have to send it to your customers manually one by one.

Go to HerPaperRoute.com/tools to see a list of the tools I recommend.

Nowadays, many payment processing platforms include sales page builders. So, if you don't have a website yet, you can sell directly through the payment processor. Though if you do have a website, now is the time to create a simple sales page for your offer.

Again, don't overthink it; just get it out there. Use a sales page template if needed. I offer some cool ones in my shop.

And that, my friend, is all there is to it. You now have a digital product created, launched, and primed to start receiving orders. The only thing left to do is promote it, which we will cover soon.

In the next chapter, we'll have an honest discussion about your brand. We'll explore the not-so-glamorous roadblocks that can hurt your progress. Things like not knowing where to start, or freezing the second you have to promote yourself. Hesitation, procrastination, and a deep-rooted fear of visibility are common blocks. They are normal and absolutely beatable. Let's unpack them together.

6

Getting Unstuck

How to Break Through the Fear and Actually Launch Your Thing

Is this you? You have *so many* ideas for your website. You spend days toying with design choices, but you've spent zero time driving traffic to your sales page. You've reworked your logo twelve times but haven't posted about your offer once. You can confidently recite your brand mission in the mirror but panic when someone asks, "So what do you do?"

If this resonates, then you might be stuck in what I call "business prep purgatory." And if so, we need to shake you out of it. Instead of spending three weeks coming up with the perfect brand mission (which, let's be real, no one remembers anyway), I implore you to do as discussed in the previous chapter and spend three hours making an offer. Then, promote it in places where your ideal customer hangs out so they can buy it. Don't make this more complicated than it needs to be.

You *do* need to think about what kind of brand you are building because this will heavily impact the future. And speaking of the future, as you're getting your website and your brand up and running, it's going to feel like a job, because it is. The trick is to find what parts of the job you enjoy doing, focus on those, and automate or outsource the rest.

Business Prep Purgatory

What if every time you think of a business idea, your mind fills with worries? Or it creates new roadblocks? You know the type, "I can't start this because I need to do these seven thousand other things before I'm ready." I get it. We've all been there. The moment you decide to start a business, your brain panics.

Suddenly, you think that you need to morph into a Fortune 500 CEO overnight. Like some sort of Mighty Morphin Power Boss. You start obsessing over mission statements, color palettes, and whether or not your brand voice is "Gen Z, yet Boomer" (um, WTF does that even mean?).

Meanwhile, your bank account is side-eyeing you like, "Bestie, do we have a groovy plan for making actual brass yet, or nah?" (Did I just nail the right combo of Gen Z and Boomer?) Let me save you some stress...business plans don't pay the bills. Sales do.

Honey, you need to stop romanticizing "business prep." It's a trap! An all-too-common dangerous dupery new entrepreneurs fall into is procrastination disguised as preparation. It feels productive to map out your entire brand story, choose the perfect font, and create a dreamy mood board for your website. If you've spent weeks perfecting your "About Page" but haven't sold anything yet, sorry, but you're caught in procrastination hell.

The truth is your brain is playing dirty and trying to sabotage you into falling for this trap. Why do you feel the need to perfect your tagline, create an elaborate website design, or write a 20-page vision statement before you "officially" start? That's procrastination in disguise. And worse, it's your sneaky imposter syndrome whispering, "If you just tweak a few more things, you'll finally be ready." It's lying to you!

Annoyingly, your brain will invent obstacles to keep you stuck in prep mode because starting is scary. It will convince you to watch "just one more webinar" before taking action. It will trick you into thinking that stressing over coming up with a website tagline is actual progress. It's not, and no one cares about your tagline—even you, if you'd be honest! The reality is that these are all little detours designed to delay the moment when you put yourself out there. Because once you start, there's a chance of failing. And that freaks your subconscious the hell out.

Oh, and surprise! The only way to feel like a *real* entrepreneur is to do entrepreneurial tasks. This means selling something! Not tweaking a logo for the fifth time that nobody else cares about.

Sophia Amoruso began selling vintage clothes on eBay without any startup cash. This venture grew into the multimillion-dollar brand Nasty Gal. She sold Nasty Gal for a reported $20 million.

Sara Blakely didn't waste time on a corporate mission statement. Instead, she used her savings to make a prototype for Spanx in her apartment, wore it herself to test it, and literally hustled her way into Neiman Marcus.

Rachel Rodgers didn't let a childhood spent surviving on food stamps define her future. She started her coaching company with a small budget, evolved it into the Hello Seven Podcast, and became the first millionaire in her family. Eight-figure millionaire, to be exact.

Or how about Jenna Kutcher? Jenna didn't start with a massive audience or perfect branding. She started the Gold Digger Podcast in her closet with a cheap microphone and grew it into a multi-million-dollar business.

These women didn't overthink it. They got scrappy, started small, and focused on selling first. Need more proof? Hello, I did the same! When I started my first monetized blog while on maternity leave, I had no startup funds, fancy website, or cool branding. My site looked like horse shit! Did I stress about that? *Neigh.*

Creating content and offers with one arm and my newborn son snuggled in the other, I bootstrapped my business from the couch. If I had allowed overthinking to get in my way, I would never have gotten my business off the ground. As a result of sticking with it, my blogging income has allowed me the financial freedom I previously only dreamed about. I've bought a home for my family, saved for my kid's education, built an emergency fund, and more, all while doing something I enjoy. This is why I am so passionate about encouraging women to take action and *start the dang thing* that's calling them.

I'm With the Brand

As you build your business, you're going to have to promote it. And this can be where people can stumble. As the face of a brand, you need to get comfortable talking about your accomplishments.

I know, I know, women are sometimes taught not to boast. To wait for someone to notice their value instead of owning it. Well, as you step into your glow-up era, that coy crap ends now.

Telling people what you've achieved is not bragging; it's one of your essential selling features. You need to share your wins, not to brag, but as proof that you know what you're doing. And, if you want a strong personal brand, talk about your work *loudly* because no one is going to magically find you otherwise.

Learn to publicly promote your offers *often*, even if you're afraid of seeming repetitive. Why? Because, like it or not, even if people want to buy from you, they need to be reminded that you exist! There's a guideline we use in marketing called The Rule of Seven. It's the principle that someone must see or hear a message at least seven times before they remember it or trust it enough to take action. Whether the message is a brand, product, sale reminder, or a person, being exposed to it seven times is considered to be what it takes before someone's mind fully takes note of it.

The next time you feel uncomfortable about self-promotion, remember this. If you had the cure for a disease, you would not hesitate to tell people about it. You'd speak up and share it. You'd do everything you could to get it into the right hands.

Well, your business also solves a problem. Maybe not a medical one, but it's still one that matters. So why are you downplaying it and keeping it a secret? The world needs more women who own what they've built and aren't afraid to talk about it.

When writing this book, I reached out to career coach Courtney Johnson to weigh in on this. She said:

"The #1 problem holding you back from your career dreams is the fear of self-promotion. We make a million excuses, thinking we'll finally promote ourselves only when we've achieved X amount in revenue or achieved whatever other arbitrary accolade that makes us 'worthy' of a personal brand. But here's the secret: you don't develop a personal brand when you achieve those goals. A personal brand is *how* you achieve them. Through self-promotion, you gain top-of-mind awareness in your audience's minds. This means you're first in line for opportunities as they come up, and these compound over time.

Realize that when you hold back from promoting yourself and sharing your expertise, you're robbing the world of YOU. You have unique value to share. Value that's filtered through your unique perspective. Which is a combination of your own learnings and experiences that no one else can fulfill but you.

Everyone has doubts, but the best gift you can give the world is to share your knowledge regardless of the doubts because it gives others the permission to create as well. If you're still unsure of building your personal brand, think of it as risk vs. reward." – Courtney Johnson @Courtney..Johnson

When you're launching a personal brand, having clarity on what makes you different is a superpower. I'm not talking vague "I help people live their best lives," I mean crystal-clear, high-definition "this is what makes me unforgettable" clarity. Yes, I know. It's hard. You might worry that there are thousands of people online doing what you do. You might think that no one will buy from you because there's already someone else selling something similar. Well, yes, there are lots of other people selling similar things as what you're offering. Sure, maybe they have cuter websites or more followers who actually comment. (Ugh, what's that like?!)

However, your differentiation isn't about being the only one. It's about *being the right one for the right people*. No one else is YOU. No one else has your unique perspective, ideas, or backstory. It is your particular flavor of brilliance and unique way of describing it that will attract the right people to you. Think about your favorite people online. They all have something that makes them different. Maybe it is their humor, their perspective, their storytelling, or something you have in common with them that makes you feel a connection. Think about a product you buy over and over. Plenty of people sell candles, but you buy the one that smells like your ex's hoodie. That's what branding does.

Your goal is to figure out what makes you unique and bring more of it into your content so that the right people can discover and connect with you. Instead of worrying about who's already doing what you do, start showing us why no one can do it quite like you. And then, use your story to sell that.

When new clients hire me for a business consultation, I send them an onboarding questionnaire. One of the questions on it is, "What made you want to work with me?" Most of the time people answer that they felt connected to me because of something weird or funny I shared in my newsletter. Nine times out of ten the story they connected with was not a business-related one, but a purely personal one. Let that sink in.

People tend to buy from people they relate to, so don't run from that. Use it to your advantage. The fastest way to make someone relate to you is to share a story. Your story does not have to be dramatic. It just has to be real. Maybe you started your business while working a nine-to-five you hated. A lot of people can relate to that. Perhaps you struggled with confidence for years before finally stepping into your power. Who hasn't felt like that at least a dozen times in life? What does your day-to-day look like? These are the stories that make people feel connected to you. That connection builds trust, and trust leads to sales.

In chapter 3, we discussed the power that words can have for your own well-being. In the same way, words play a powerful part when you talk about or describe your brand and in people's decisions to open their wallets or not. For example, instead of telling someone, "I sell social media templates for small businesses," try, "When I started my first business, I had no idea how to create content that actually got social media engagement. I spent hours, frustrated, trying to make graphics. Now I create done-for-you templates so business owners like you don't have to go through that struggle." One sounds like a product. The other sounds like a person helping another person solve a problem. Both are true, but the second version involves the listener—and that's the magic pixie dust.

Another important point is that if you're building a personal brand, really consider how your audience perceives you. And no, your brand is not your logo, your fonts, or your feed. Your brand is the feeling people get when they think about you/your business, especially when you're not in the room. Take a step back and look at your brand through your audience's eyes. What story are you actually telling? It might surprise you. It might sting a little. But when you really understand how people perceive you, you can start shaping your brand with intention.

Realize that what you think about your brand might not be exactly how others see it. Everything you say, post, and do filters into an image of your brand in the minds of your audience. This is why knowing and controlling your brand's voice and having a consistent writing and design style matter. Otherwise, what's your brand whispering behind your back?

Now that you know how to build a personal brand, here is your action plan:

1. Write down what makes you different. Define your vibe, story, and unique angle.

2. Recall the struggles and setbacks you've experienced.

3. Then, start sharing your story. Post about how you got started, what you've overcome, and what you have learned. Talk about your wins, your process, and how you help people.

4. Show up consistently. Your brand is not built in a day. But if you keep showing up, being real, and sharing value,

people will start paying attention.

Also, hot tip: Please PLEASE hire a professional photographer to take your branding photos. You might think a selfie is good enough, but to a potential customer, it's not. Get some professional headshots. Thank me later.

Building a Personal Brand vs. Faceless Brand

So, you've got your idea. You're setting up your website. You're officially building a brand. Hooray! Now comes a huge decision: Are you going to build a personal brand where you are the face of the business? Or are you creating a faceless brand that can operate (and eventually sell) without being tied to you? This choice matters a lot. Because the way you structure your brand now will impact a number of things, like your ability to scale, your workload, and whether or not you can sell it later. So, let's break it down. What's the difference between a personal brand and a non-personal brand?

A Personal Brand

You are the business. Your name, face, and reputation are the brand. People follow it because of your personality, expertise, or unique perspective. Your credibility, voice, and content drive the business. The key points about a personal brand are:

- **Best for:** Coaches, speakers, consultants, influencers, authors, course creators, and thought leaders.

- **Pros:** Faster trust-building, as people connect with people. It may be easier to make money at first, especially when selling trust-based products like courses or coaching services.

- **Biggest downsides:** It's harder to sell this kind of business later because the business is built around you and your persona. If you leave, the brand loses its biggest asset (you). Also, scaling is harder because you have to be "on" all the time, which means it's difficult to separate your work and personal life. Also, no anonymity! Everything you publish is attached to your name.

A Faceless Brand

This is a business that runs without your persona. Think: The Everygirl, BuzzFeed, The Cut, or any niche blog that doesn't have a single face attached to it. The business has its own brand identity separate from you. You can build content, products, and services without being the main attraction. The key points about a faceless brand include:

- **Best for:** Blogs, e-commerce stores, media sites, software companies, niche websites, and agencies.

- **Pros:** A faceless brand is easier to sell later because it's not dependent on you. It's also easier to scale because you can outsource, automate, and grow without you being the bottleneck. As the owner, you have more privacy and don't have be "on" 24/7. This brand can be easier to monetize with ad revenue.

- **Biggest downsides:** It takes longer to build trust in a faceless brand since people connect with people more than with logos, and it may require more branding and marketing efforts.

Are you building a personal brand where your face, name, and expertise are front and center? Or are you creating a brand that can run independently of you and can eventually be sold to someone new? Either one can be a smart move. The key is knowing which model supports your long-term goals.

Personally, I own multiple websites. Some are faceless brands that I built with the sole intent to flip them later. They're creative outlets where I can write anonymously and test different monetization strategies. These businesses give me creative freedom while still making money in the background. Later, I'll sell them.

Then, I have my personal brand, Chelsea Clarke, founder of HerPaperRoute, the one you're engaging with right now. This is where I build credibility in my industry, make connections, and teach others what I've learned. I also have a home decor blog where I share my renovation progress. I don't plan on selling either of these.

OK, so how do you choose which option is right for you right now? Ask yourself:

- Will I enjoy being the "face" of my business? If yes, → personal brand.

If no, → faceless brand.

- Do I want to be recognized as an expert in my field? If yes, → personal brand.
  If no, → faceless brand.

- Do I want creative freedom without being tied to my name? If yes, → faceless brand. If no, → personal brand.

- Do I want to sell this business one day? If yes, → build a faceless, sellable brand.

Still unsure which way to go? You can do both by operating multiple websites. Keep your personal brand for authority and credibility. Build faceless brands as assets you can sell later. That's exactly what I do. The key is knowing what you want long-term.

If there's one thing I want you to take away from this section, it's this. Be intentional about the kind of business you're building. Otherwise, here's what happens when people don't plan: Someone starts a personal brand, thinking it's easy. Soon, she finds she can't sell it, escape it, or take a vacation without it falling apart. Another woman builds a faceless brand but gets frustrated that it takes longer to build trust and an audience. She wastes years creating content, monetizing half-heartedly, and running in circles because she never actually decided what she wanted from this business in the first place.

That's not going to be you. You're taking the time to think this through. You're building your business with the end game in mind. There is no wrong choice here. The only mistake is not deciding and hoping it all magically works out.

So, if you're building a personal brand, own it. Be the face of your business, show up consistently, and monetize with high-value offers that leverage your unique voice and expertise. If you love being the face of your business and don't mind showing up on camera, a personal brand could be your power move.

Or, if you value privacy and an exit strategy, build a faceless business that can be sold later, something that makes money without needing you 24/7. Think like an investor, and build something that can run without you. If you're building a faceless brand, create a strong, recognizable brand identity. Focus on evergreen traffic and revenue, and structure it so that one day, someone else can buy it and keep it running without you. The choice is yours!

The Consistency Phase and Dealing with Creator's Block

Every business owner, creative, entrepreneur, or successful person you admire has faced creator's block. Most often, they didn't have a special moment where motivation struck, and they suddenly felt like doing the hard things. They just did them anyway. Maybe they did feel that spark at the beginning when they felt the initial thrill of starting something. But probably not when it came to the hard part, the tedious and boring work that is required to actually finish the job after its sparkly inception. You know, *the consistency phase.*

This is the phase many may not think about when they start a business. Once you've got your offer and an audience, you can't just sit idly and hope it sells itself. To get off the ground, there needs to be consistent effort. Even when you're tired, unmotivated, and full of self-doubt. As creators, we can't wait for inspiration. We have to do our work regardless.

Want to launch a digital product? Make the first draft today, even if it's ugly. Want to go viral on social media? Press record and start yappin'. Want to get in shape? Go for a walk. Want to grow your audience? Post something. Anything. Stop overthinking. You don't need to feel ready. You need to start acting like the kind of person who does the work, even if you don't feel inspired.

Creator's block (AKA writer's block) is that brick wall that erects itself right on top of the part of your brain you use for making thoughts the moment you finally sit down to create content. One day, you're bursting with ideas while shampooing your hair. The next, you've watched a blinking cursor for *hours*, unable to imagine a single word. What I do know is that creator's block is not a sign that you're a talentless hack or that your business is doomed. It's just that your brain is being dramatic.

When I'm stuck, my brain likes to try to distract me from my work, especially when I have a deadline! I'll be working on a new product launch, and that little voice will say, Hey, we should *totally* debate the font size on our website right now! Should it be between 19px and 20px? Let's spend the next six days focusing on this. Sound familiar?

Now that I am aware of this all too common trickery we play on ourselves, I've got a tactic to combat it. Whenever I catch my brain pulling such shenanigans, I immediately call it out. I'll acknowledge that she's being a distracting diva, tell her to knock it off, and then shift focus back to the task.

This is not easy for someone who has ADHD, but the acknowledging part really helps. As does treating her(my brain) like its own character outside of myself. Don't let your brain trick you into busy work. Call its bluff and take action instead. You are calling the shots here; you are the boss. You have to get back to the task at hand even when you don't feel like it.

You might be thinking, "Okay, Chelsea, I know I need to act even when I don't want to. But *what* should I do when I feel stuck?"

Here's how we're going to get you into a good headspace right now before you sit down to your creative work today.

1. **Go for a walk outside**. Take 10 minutes and get out of your house. Ten minutes of fresh air is key. Don't try to force any creative ideas while on this walk. The point is just to experience the walk and let your thoughts wander however they like.

2. **Talk it out like you're talking to a friend**. Open Google Docs on your phone and click the little microphone, and start blabbing about your business like you're explaining it to your bestie over coffee. The app will transcribe everything you say as you say it. BOOM! Content. You can literally turn your voice into text. The future is wild.

3. **Lower the bar (like, all the way down)**. There's a good chance you're stuck because you think your work has to be *brilliant, groundbreaking, life-changing, Pulitzer-worthy* perfection. It doesn't. Your first draft should be absolute trash. Just get words, ideas, or actions *out*. You can refine them later. Bad writing is the gateway to good writing. The point is to just get something, literally any hot garbage, onto the page. Later, you'll go back and add your personality.

4. **Ask your audience what they need**. This is so simple. Go straight to the source. Post a simple story on Instagram and ask, "What's your biggest struggle with XYZ?" You'll be given instant content prompts straight from your audience. They'll tell you exactly what they want, so you don't have to sit there guessing.

5. **Lie to yourself about the existence of time**. This is such a great life hack (which you met in chapter 4), and I do it all the time. Tell yourself you'll just do *five minutes*. Five minutes of writing, brainstorming, moving, and creating. Once you start, you'll probably keep going.

But most importantly, stop waiting for perfect conditions to get down to business, will ya? You don't need the perfect desk setup. You don't need a free day with zero distractions. You don't need motivation, or clarity, or a "good idea." You just need to start messy and figure it out as you go.

Finally, remember that, literally, no one is analyzing your content as hard as you are. Your audience is not sitting there with a red pen, judging every word. They just want value. Give them that, post the thing, and move on with your life.

Creator's block isn't an actual wall. It's just you getting in your own way. Now it's time to create. So lower the stakes and go make something. And if it sucks? Congratulations, you're officially in the game.

7

Trust Yourself, but Build a Community

Collaboration Over Competition and Why Community Matters for Your Brand

When I married my husband only a few weeks after meeting him, it was because I knew it was right. We did not wait the appropriate amount of time so that society would deem it reasonable. It wasn't logical or part of some well-thought-out five-year plan. My intuition *simply knew,* and so did his.

Intuition is your guiding light in life and business. You have to trust yourself. I've learned that the best decisions you'll ever make are often the ones that don't make sense to anyone but you. And this doesn't apply to only love. It applies to your business, career, and entire life. That "crazy" business idea? It might be the thing that sets you free. That online business you've seen in the marketplace, and you wonder if you should be the person to acquire it? It could change everything.

Everyone else might think you're wild, impulsive, and unrealistic. That's fine. It's not their life. What's a risk to them could be a prominent stepping stone for you. The most successful people don't wait for anyone's approval of their ideas. They don't wait for certainty. They trust themselves. They make moves before they feel fully ready and bet on their instincts.

"But Chelsea, I heard that 50% of new businesses fail." Yeah? Well, with that logic, I heard that 50% of people who start a gym membership quit within six months. Does that mean you should never exercise again and accept your fate as a sentient couch cushion? No!

Successful people don't listen to statistics. They live by the phrase, "Statistics don't apply to me," and then they do the work they need to do. They take accountability for their own lives and don't second-guess their plans because someone else didn't succeed at theirs. *Statistics don't apply to you*. Feel it. What if I had let doubt in, if I had waited too long, or questioned my blog as a career? What if I had overanalyzed every possible outcome? Well, I wouldn't have the life I have today.

A crucial key to success is to trust your intuition, that quiet, bossy little voice that says, "This is it," or "Something feels off," or "Run. Now." It will guide you to the right opportunities. No matter whether you bought your business or built it yourself, trust your gut.

You can learn strategies, hire coaches, and binge every course under the sun. Yet, at the end of the day, it's your gut that's going to sound the alarm when something doesn't feel right. When a buyer lowballs you. When a brand deal feels off. When an idea for your next offer keeps tapping on your brain like, "Hey girl, it's me. Your million-dollar idea." Intuition is data. It's not fluff. It's not irrational. It's your subconscious processing the patterns, cues, and wisdom you've collected. Way faster than your logical brain can.

We often learn to ignore our instincts. We doubt ourselves and seek approval from others before acting. As if there's some committee of grown-ups that has righteous power to permit our desires and tell us what we should do. Sorry, but there is no committee of almighty grown-ups! Your inner voice is the one guiding you. I know you didn't come this far to let your inner voice be drowned out by what your friends, your parents, or some guy on a podcast think you should do. You came here to build something real, aligned, profitable, and *yours*.

So, if you feel a yes in your gut, even if it looks crazy on paper? Trust it and explore it. If your stomach turns every time you open your inbox to deal with a certain client or project? Trust that, too. The more you practice listening to your inner voice, the louder it gets. The coolest thing is you'll soon realize that you've known what to do all along. You only needed to trust yourself. So what is it you're hesitating on?

Content is Queen

Content creation is your golden ticket to attracting an audience. If you think about it, you most likely discovered your favorite entrepreneur, expert, or brand because of something they posted online in a blog post, video, podcast, TikTok, or an Instagram reel. Maybe it was a compelling ad. Either way, they created valuable content, you discovered them, and now here you are. Your audience will find you the same way. Content is queen.

The cool thing is that there are many, many ways to go about using content to sell your offer. I could fill ten books with the marketing strategies I've explored, and that would only scratch the surface. I don't need to overwhelm you with options, so let's focus on a solid five solid avenues of content marketing. You can cherry-pick the ones that resonate. Here are five ways to market your new offer that I believe are worth trying.

Pinterest

Number one is Pinterest. Yes, Pinterest is my favorite marketing tool, and it has been for many years. Maybe up until now, you've only ever used Pinterest as a consumer to discover and save inspiration for outfits, home decorating, recipes, and so on. However, you may not realize that Pinterest is a big curated shopping destination. To a regular user, it feels like entertainment, but to a creator, it's business. Those ideas that inspired you most likely led you to buy something at some point, right? Well, the creators who posted those images got paid, either for an affiliate commission, a full sale, or by way of ad revenue when you visited their website.

So now you get to be on the creator side and start earning from Pinterest, too. Before I explain how to do that, let's clarify that Pinterest is not like other social media platforms; in fact, it's not a social media platform at all! Instead, Pinterest is a search engine. That means you don't have to worry about trying to grow followers or get a bunch of likes. Followers and likes aren't that important when it comes to success on this platform.

Instead, you can focus your efforts on Search Engine Optimization (SEO) to ensure your pins (visual bookmarks with links) show up in search results, which will result in more traffic to your sales pages and blog posts. The goal of using this platform for your business's pins to rank high in search results so that when people search for the thing you offer, your pins come up on the first or second pages, and you get free traffic.

People go to Pinterest to find inspiration, solutions, and shopping recommendations. They are actively searching for ideas, tutorials, and things to buy. Your objective now is to make sure your offer is what they find.

Put it into action: Use Pinterest's own Trends tool to maximize your results. First, find trending topics and keywords. Next, create pins and upload them to Pinterest. When filling out the pin title and description, include the trending keywords you found a moment ago. Include a link to your sales page (or blog post) so that when people click your pin, it takes them to where you want them to go. I recommend publishing a few pins every day.

Pinterest provides some keyword data inside its Trends tool. But there are also some great third-party keyword tools that provide even more data. Discover them at HerPaperRoute.com/tools.

Content Marketing

Next, blogging is my second favorite way to convert sales to an offer. If you have a website, start publishing articles on topics related to your offer, providing practical answers to what your ideal customers want to know. This is called content marketing. Blogging, podcasting, and vlogging are all forms of content marketing. Again, don't overcomplicate it; it's simply selling things by being helpful. A content creator's job is to create content that entertains, educates, and inspires people, helping them make shopping decisions. Give value, build trust, and your audience will buy from you. People who find you through your content are already warmed up to what you are selling. You are not chasing them; they are coming to you.

This is how you can embody "I don't chase, I attract" energy. It also positions you as an authority who can solve your readers' problems. Who are you more likely to buy from? A random person shoving a product in your face? Or someone who has already helped you, answered your questions, and made your life easier for free? Exactly.

Put it into action: Write and publish blog posts on topics related to your offer, niche, and customers' needs and interests. Consider starting a podcast or YouTube channel.

You don't have to start from scratch! As will be discussed in the next chapter in detail, you can always buy an established business, one that comes with articles, traffic, customers, and subscribers.

Take a look at the businesses for sale at NicheInvestor.com to preview what's available in the market today.

Email Marketing

My third must-have marketing tool is email marketing. Email marketing is a fancy term for having a newsletter. Send valuable emails to your audience, keep them entertained and happy, and you'll have customers for the long haul.

Having an email list is also a worthy insurance policy for your business. Why? Well, if social media disappeared tomorrow or you lost access to your social accounts, would you still have a way to reach your audience? No. So, this is why having an email list and putting effort into email marketing are such vital pieces of the puzzle.

Put it into action: Start your email list today. Sign up for an email service provider and post the sign-up form or link on your website and social media. Create an opt-in freebie to give your audience in exchange for their email address. This can be anything, so long as it's something valuable and in line with your paid offer. Send a weekly newsletter where you tell stories. People love getting to know the creator behind the brand.

Social Media

Next on the list is social media. No, you do not need to be on every platform. And you do not need to post every day, either. You just need to pick one or two platforms and share helpful, entertaining, or inspiring content. The best way to tackle social media marketing is to be willing to experiment. Pay attention to how other people are using it, notice trends, and have fun with it.

Advertising and Promoted Content

Finally, paid ads and promoted pins. Ads can be a fast way to bring attention to your offer. The benefit of paying for views is that it instantly gets your offer in front of new people. Unlike the other four organic tools I mentioned, this option costs money.

I would highly suggest that you hold off paying for ads for your offer until you've made some organic sales. If your sales page is not converting organically, ads will not fix it. Ads only work when your offer is already proven. However, once it is selling organically, investing in paid ads might be an option to consider to ramp things up.

Start slow with a small budget, test and tweak, and gradually increase your ad spend. Personally, I like to run ads around specific holidays when I know people are more likely to buy something, as opposed to running the same offer forever. Your situation could be different. So, take time to test different ads to see what converts best for you.

Building a Community

Surprise! Your brand is not just about what you sell. It's about what people think of you/your business when you're not in the room. Going deeper, it's about who you bring together, the conversations you start, and the sense of belonging you create. A loyal community transforms casual followers into lifelong customers. It makes your business important to people, turning one-time buyers into brand advocates.

Community is what makes life meaningful. Having a solid friend group, a strong family connection, or just being the kind of person who says hi to their neighbors (instead of pretending not to see them) are the things that matter. As you build your business, you will realize that community is just as crucial in entrepreneurship as it is in life.

Of course, you need an audience of people to sell to if you want to make money online. Straight facts. No audience = no customers. No customers = no sales. No sales = you, sad. We don't want that! But here's where most people get stuck. They assume "finding an audience" means desperately spamming social media with offers 24/7. Or, worse, they think they have to become an influencer. Or wait until they have a massive following before they can start selling. None of that is true.

If you are stopping yourself from posting because you're scared of looking like an influencer, I have words for you. I know what that fear *really* is. You're not scared to look like an influencer; you're scared to be seen *failing at attempting* to be an influencer. The truth is that working in the creator economy does not mean having to be an influencer at all. Likewise, posting content on social media does not mean you are trying to be an influencer.

Take me, for example; I post content for brand awareness and opportunities. That's it. I have a message to share with the world, so I share it. And I don't care if someone thinks I'm trying to be an influencer or failing at being an influencer. Because I know I'm not. I'm simply focused on gaining more visibility for my business and attracting more opportunities. What anyone else sees is none of my business.

Earlier, we chatted about creating your offer. Hopefully, you followed the steps I gave you, and you now have something available for sale on the Internet. If so, great! You did an amazing job. That's part one. The easy part. The second part is where the real work begins.

It's time to promote your offer. Things don't sell themselves, so to actually get conversions, you need to market it. The right marketing is how you go from, "I hope someone buys this," to "Wow, I need to hire an assistant to handle all these sales." Don't let the word *marketing* scare you! It can be as complicated or as simple as you want it to be. I like to do it the simple way. You won't catch me spending weeks agonizing over competitor analysis reports or using stupid words like "omnichannel strategy." I see marketing as a basic means to an end: It puts the offer in front of the people who want it. It's that simple.

Ultimately, regardless of how slick your marketing plan is, if no one sees your offer, it doesn't exist. So, this stage is super important. Know that you don't need to be a marketing expert to sell your offer successfully. You just need to understand where your ideal customer hangs out and put your offer in their line of sight.

Here's what I mean by this. Let's say you've just acquired a food blog, and you want to create an offer that complements the blog. So, you decide to create an ebook of easy air fryer recipes. Not only will you earn by selling the ebook, but you've also added the affiliate links of your favorite air fryers to the inside of the book. This is great. You've monetized your offer in multiple ways. Now, we need people to discover it. You'll want to create some evergreen content for your ebook, such as pinning content about it on Pinterest and publishing blog posts on your website that promote it. Maybe you'll mention your ebook on your TikTok or Instagram whenever you post a new video.

Let's also consider the time of year. Can we capitalize on seasonal trends? When are most people buying air fryers? I would guess that it is usually Christmas in the winter and Amazon Prime Day in the summer. So, I would make sure you are live-posting in air fryer and foodie-focused Facebook groups and Reddit threads during these times. Why? Because this is when people are most likely to look up ideas for what they can do with their new air fryer.

Doing what, you ask? You could post helpful content about air fryer recipes, answer people's questions about using air fryers, and start polls on users' air fryer experiences with the CTA being the link to your ebook sales page. Don't overthink it; just go where your customers are and be useful to them.

People don't merely buy products; *they buy belonging*. They want to be seen and heard and feel like they're part of something bigger than just another sales funnel. And that's where your community comes in. Building a loyal audience around your business isn't about shouting into the void of the Internet and hoping someone throws money at you. It's about creating a space where people feel so connected to you and your brand that they'd follow you into battle (or at least to your next product launch).

Before I had an offer, before I had a proper website, and definitely before I had a clue what I was doing, I knew one thing: I needed to build a community first. So, I did the simplest, most effective thing I could think of. I set up a landing page, invited people to join my email list, and gave them something valuable as a welcome gift: a photo pack they could use in their businesses. No fluff, no big promises, just a simple, "Hey, I made this for you; come hang out."

Then, I showed up every single week in their inboxes. I sent newsletters that felt like catching up with a friend over coffee, where I told stories about my daily life alongside business tips. These story-based newsletters made my audience of home-based business owners feel like they belonged to something bigger *because they do!* I talked about my niche, answered questions, and shared my real, sometimes messy "figuring-it-out-as-I-go" journey.

Something incredible happened: People stuck around. They started replying to my emails, engaging with my content, and genuinely wanting to be part of what I was building. Even though I wasn't selling anything yet. I had created *comfort content*, something positive that people looked forward to reading. That was the secret sauce!

By the time I launched my first product, I didn't have to beg for sales. My community was already excited to support me because I had spent months supporting them. This is the power of a community-first business. It's not about transactional relationships. Rather, it's about giving before you ask, building trust, and making people feel like they're part of something cool.

The best thing is that selling becomes effortless when people feel like they're part of something. Not just being marketed to. Your community is your hype squad and your ride-or-dies. They share your business with friends, celebrate your wins, and stay with you. Even if your first product launch flops or you send a promo email with "Insert Discount Code Here" still in it, they've got your back.

When you show up and provide value, your audience becomes the main character in your brand's story. This creates something much bigger than just the product. I believe that when you prioritize connection over conversion, you never have to convince people to buy from you. They're already invested. They want you to win because they feel like they're winning, too.

So, how do you create a community? Here's a step-by-step system that has worked for me. I have used these four simple steps to build multiple thriving newsletters and grow engaged communities.

Step 1: Give people a reason to care

Creating an offer and putting it up for sale is the foundation of your business. The next step, if you want to take your offer to new heights is to build a community around your brand. People who genuinely hype it up, keep purchasing, and refer your products to their friends.

To do this, you need to give your customers a reason to care, beyond the offer itself. What's the vibe, mission, transformation it represents for people? This is the difference between brands with die-hard communities and others that are just...there.

For example, people are not buying a bottle of face serum. They're buying the confidence that comes with glowing skin. They are not buying a fitness plan. They are buying the feeling of strength, energy, and self-respect. They are not buying a coaching program. They are buying clarity, direction, and the belief that success is possible.

When you build a brand that makes people feel seen and understood, they become more than customers. They turn into fans, advocates, ambassadors, and repeat buyers. If you don't know yet why people would want to stick around your brand, ask:

- Why would someone feel like this is a community?
- What do they get *beyond your product*?
- What makes your business feel like home?
- What values, beliefs, and personality do you bring?
- What do you stand for that makes people say, "Hell yes, I need this in my life"?

When you figure that out, make it loud and clear. Your audience should know exactly what they're signing up for when they follow you.

Step 2. Show Up Like a Human

Nobody—and I mean nobody—wants to follow a brand that sounds like a corporate robot vomiting marketing jargon. You know the type. The ones that say things like, "Leverage cutting-edge strategies to optimize core competencies and maximize ROI." Stop. Just stop. People connect with humans. They follow humans. They buy from humans. I always say talk to your audience like you would a best friend, not a potential sale.

Show up as yourself. Be funny. Be real. Share your wins but also the facepalm-worthy mistakes that got you there. Let people see the behind-the-scenes chaos of building your business, the messy drafts, the failed launches, the moment you realize you spelled your own brand name wrong on a product label.

Take this book, for example. If I had only shared business advice and left out my personal stories and mistakes, this would be a pretty boring read, right? You'd skim a few pages, nod politely, and then forget it ever existed. Yet because I am telling you the real, messy, behind-the-scenes version of how I built my business, you're more likely to care.

Your audience will feel the same way about your brand. If you want people to stick around, give them something to connect with. Be human. It's the best marketing strategy you'll ever use.

Step 3: Create Spaces for Connection and Make Your People Feel Seen

We know that people want to interact, connect, and feel like they're part of something bigger, so curate a place where they can. What can you create to provide spaces for them to interact, share, and build relationships beyond just following your brand?

How about a private membership where they get exclusive content? Sort of like the VIP lounge of your brand. Maybe you can host monthly "office hours" where you show up on Zoom to answer their questions and create a real-time connection. Or how about something more asynchronous, like a Facebook group or Slack channel?

Adding personal touches like, "Reply to this email and share your day," at the end of your newsletter helps people feel valued. It shows them they're chatting with a real person, not just a brand. Shout out your customers. Feature them. Respond to their DMs and comments. Truly, nothing turns a casual reader into a superfan faster than feeling like the creator they follow actually notices them.

Step 4: Build in Public

Building in public means that you share the journey of what you're working on for all to see as it develops. Working on a new course? Take your audience along for the ride as you create it. Show them how you're building it. Give them a behind-the-scenes view of all the stages of production. With each view, they grow more curious about what you're offering and are more likely to want to buy it, because they trust you, know you, and have been along for the ride watching you build it. Finally, here's the best-kept secret in business: When you build an engaged, loyal community, selling never feels like selling. You don't have to beg, chase, or awkwardly slide into people's DMs with a "Hey girl!" You know what your audience likes, and you make yourself useful to them.

By the time you are ready to open your shopping cart, your offer won't be a surprise to your audience. Rather, they will be eager to be able to obtain it finally!

So, focus on building your inner circle of future customers, clients, and brand ambassadors. Be consistent, share yourself, and don't be afraid to let them see the messy, relatable side of you.

Girlhood

I wasn't always a girl's girl. Yes, I've always had close female friendships that I valued immensely, but when I was younger, considering the other girls in situations wasn't always my first thought. I am a girl's girl now, thank Goddess. But it's something I had to actually learn how to be as an adult after being exposed to a LOT of toxic programming my entire life (hello, every teen movie ever). Stuff that took much unlearning.

Growing up, sadly, I believed that other girls were competition. Competition for popularity, for rank, for boys, for attention. I was deep in my "I'm not like other girls" era, side-eyeing anything too feminine, believing that standing out meant standing apart from other females.

Consciously or unconsciously, I thought that getting attention and approval from males was something to strive for. Dare I say it? There were times when I acted like a "pick me." How utterly embarrassing!

If you've ever been a pick me, if you've ever chased male validation, or chosen a guy's word over a woman's, don't beat yourself up. Maybe you laughed at a terrible, misogynistic joke just to appear cool around the guys. We've all been there. Seriously, show me a woman who hasn't, at some point, uttered the words "I just get along better with guys," or "Girls are too much drama," or pretended to like fantasy football, and I'll show you a unicorn.

It's not your fault; it's the system we've been forced into since birth. Almost every type of media has conditioned us to avoid being girl's girls. From the time we are little, media plants a message so deep in our subconscious that we barely notice it: Your worth is tied to male approval.

It starts early. Fairy tales, princess movies, and childhood storybooks shape how we see ourselves and our role in the world. Cinderella, Snow White, and Sleeping Beauty were all passive heroines whose "happily ever after" is entirely dependent on being chosen by a prince. They do not do much to change their own fate. They wait, suffer, and endure until a man decides they are worthy of rescuing.

Or how about *The Little Mermaid*, where Ariel literally gives up her voice for a chance at being with a man? If that is not the most on-the-blowhole metaphor for women being conditioned to silence themselves for male validation, I do not know what is. Modern reality dating shows where dozens of women compete for the attention of one man do not help this narrative, either.

By the time we become adults, such messages are deeply ingrained in us. They shape our thoughts and actions. Shaping how we see ourselves, how we interact with other women, and what we believe makes us valuable. When really, we should be prioritizing female friendships and celebrating girlhood. The good news is, you can snap out of it and reclaim your power anytime.

Finding love is a beautiful thing, but we need healthy relationship depictions in media, like more plotlines based around friendship rather than romance. Stories where the payoff isn't a kiss or an engagement ring but a celebration of best friends. Can we please have more movies and shows depicting healthy, platonic friendships for women with women, men with men, and women with men? I think our society would be better off.

Reclaiming Girl Power

Years ago, while getting my makeup done on a music video set, I had an interaction that changed how I see other women forever. A beautiful (and I mean intimidatingly beautiful) woman took the seat beside me and waited for the makeup artist.

Usually, when two women who don't know each other find themselves in a room together, they don't speak, especially on set, where everyone is competing for screen time. But she immediately turned to me and introduced herself warmly. We started chatting. It was refreshing to meet someone chill enough to strike up a conversation in a situation like this.

Then, as if reading my mind, she said, "I always make sure I introduce myself to pretty girls. I used to feel really scared around other women and would not open up and be friendly. Like I was scared that they'd be mean to me if I said hi."

"Oh my god, I know exactly what you mean!" I sighed. "Honestly, if you hadn't said hi first, I might have just sat here silently, thinking you'd be mean too!"

She laughed, "Yeah, like, why can't we all just get along and be friends out here?" She was so right. And by "out here," I knew she did not mean only on the set of music videos. She meant everywhere. Out here in the world.

Through my work building my woman-centric business, I've learned to celebrate female success and relationships above all. I found my way back to girlhood, and there's no way I'll ever lose my membership card again. In doing so, I realized a big reason why our society really doesn't want us to be girl's girls.

The society we live in, ahem, the patriarchy, does not want women congregating. It does not want us building each other up, forming unbreakable bonds, or, heaven forbid, realizing just how powerful we are when we stop competing and start collaborating. It would much rather keep us distracted, divided, and doubting each other because the moment we come together? They fear we'll take over.

Think about it. Why are women called "basic" when we like things that are popular? Loving our Stanley mugs just means we have a shared interest and something that connects us. Why are girly things dismissed as dumb, frivolous, or a waste of time? Gossip, brunch dates, book clubs, the color pink, and even something as simple as a group chat filled with women hyping each other up are all put down as trivial.

Why? Because these things allow us to create connection and support and to share knowledge, resources, and strategies. Which is dangerous to a system that thrives on women staying small, isolated, insecure, and dependent. Men, making business deals on the golf course? That's networking. Women bonding over coffee and swapping career advice? That's frivolous chatter. Men, forming powerful old boys' clubs to keep each other rich? That's just how the world works. Women, creating sisterhoods to uplift each other? That's cliquey and "dramatic." Do you see the pattern?

Here's the real tea. Women have been passing down wisdom, resources, and strategies since the dawn of time. Through whispers, gossip, and so-called witchcraft. Women coming together, whether in business, in friendship, or for a crusade, is a direct threat to a world that has spent centuries pitting us against each other.

That's why they turned gossip into a dirty word when, in reality, gossip has been a survival tool for women since the beginning of time. It's how we've warned each other about unsafe men, shady employers, poison forest berries, and other dangers hidden in plain sight. It's how we've passed down wisdom, built support systems, and protected each other when no one else would.

Patriarchal society tries hard to make sure we stay suspicious of each other, envious of each other, and too distracted by competing to realize we should be teaming up and running this whole show. So what do we do? We gather anyway. We hype each other up louder. We reclaim the power of girl talk, girl time, and girl gangs. The more we link arms, the harder we are to control. This is our collective power.

I stopped seeing other women as rivals and started seeing them as the greatest source of strength, power, and support imaginable. The more I connected with women in business, the more I saw our power as collaborators. When I started embracing girlhood again in a way that reclaimed all the things I once dismissed, it all made sense. I stopped rolling my eyes at softness, at whimsy, at the beauty of femininity.

Now, I love celebrating all that makes us uniquely powerful: Our intuition, our ability to create, and our knack for lifting each other up even when the world tries to push us down. There is nothing more freeing than unlearning the lie that we have to do this alone. There is nothing more powerful than choosing collaboration over competition. Celebrating each other's wins instead of feeling threatened by them is mighty.

This is why I built my company, HerPaperRoute. I know what it's like to feel stuck, underestimated, and without a community. I created what I needed: a space for women creators. Here, you get real guidance, fluff-free strategies, and a community that won't let you play small.

Through my blog, podcast, and private membership community, I help women break out of the nice-girl mindset, ditch financial dependence, and step into their power as creators, entrepreneurs, and CEOs. Because when women own their income, their voices, and their confidence, society has no choice but to adjust. If you're vibing with this, pop over to HerPaperRoute.com to discover how you can get involved in the community.

So now, allow me to make this crystal clear. I love being like other girls! I love my iced coffee. I love the color pink and catching up with other women over chips and guac. I love frilly socks, friendship bracelets, little dogs, and matching workout sets. Girls are the coolest.

Let's make so-called girly things powerful again. Let's embrace the "basic" things that we enjoy. Let's stop downplaying the magic of women gathering, laughing, strategizing, and celebrating each other. Girlhood is the best community. The more we come together, the less someone else can control us and the more collective power we own.

8

Leveling Up

Website Investing: Acquire, Scale, Exit

Here's the secret most new business owners miss: A business is an asset. It's not just a website, an Instagram page, or a side hustle; it's something that can grow in value over time. If you build it right and have the right systems in place, it becomes something you can sell for a profit.

In fact, websites are often bought and sold. That's what I do. Did you know that instead of building your own website, you could buy an existing one for your business? Even if selling your business isn't on your mind now, that could change in a few years. I see it often! That's why it's so important to have an exit plan from the beginning so you can maximize your sales price. We are glowing up your current reality here but also laying the path so your future self can continue to glow up in her reality, too.

Starting with an Exit Strategy

If you want to set yourself up for the biggest possible payday down the road, you need to think like an investor from day one.

That means treating your business like something that will eventually change hands, whether that is two years from now or twenty.

Shortly after I got married, I was hired at a business brokerage. Business brokers are like real estate agents, but for selling people's businesses, not homes. I worked in the marketing department. My job was to build listing pages, design marketing deliverables, and manage the company's social media and newsletter. Before getting hired there, I had taken an interest in the idea of buying a business. Often, I would scroll on business-for-sale websites late at night, imagining what it would be like to own a laundromat or a restaurant. So when I saw that the firm had a job opening in the marketing department, I thought, why not apply?

Well, I ended up learning a lot about the mergers and acquisitions industry there, and it sparked a new curiosity in me. A curiosity that would lead to a whole new passion and life mission later. Working at the office, I grew to admire the business brokers; their career paths seemed intriguing.

I wasn't interested in selling brick-and-mortar businesses as they did. Instead, I saw an opportunity in digital business acquisitions. Do people want to buy and sell online businesses? Could I help them do it? Yes, yes they do. And yes, yes I can. I wanted to learn as much as possible, so I enrolled in a business broker training program at the International Business Brokers Association. The program focused only on brick-and-mortar businesses, nothing digital. That said, I took what I learned and vowed to apply it to the online space one day.

As the owner of a business, no matter how big or small, many issues can arise if you don't have an exit plan. This is why I teach my clients to start their businesses with an exit strategy in place from the start. Even if you don't think you'll sell one day! So how is this done?

It starts by structuring your business so that, if and when the time comes, you can sell it for top dollar. To begin with, use a business name, not your own. Instead of "Amanda's Squirrel Befriending Tips," go with something like "Squirrel Friends." Also, create products that don't require you. Earn from templates, memberships, digital products, affiliate commissions, ad revenue, and so on. Don't just sell services, as a new owner would have to know how to perform those services too. If you intend to sell your business one day, here are some additional tips.

Finances in Order

First and foremost, keep records of everything. You want to make sure that you keep your financial records neat and tidy. While working at that brokerage, I got to see every client's financial records. Little me, with a front-row view of just how complicated selling a business can be if the company's records aren't immaculate. A business with messy, unclear finances is a business that is hard to sell, plain and simple.

Buyers want to see accurate numbers, consistent revenue, and a clear profit margin. I recommend keeping a monthly profit and loss spreadsheet so you have an at-a-glance overview of what you're spending and what you're earning. If you have been mixing personal and business expenses under one account, please stop! Open a separate business bank account so you can track everything properly. Buyers will not want to dig through your Venmo history trying to separate business income from brunch receipts.

So, keep your finances spotless. Set up systems that make your business a no-brainer for someone to buy. When it's time to sell, you don't want to beg for buyers. You don't want to appear desperate—like you need someone to take the business off your hands. Rather, you want potential buyers lining up, eager to grab what you've built. That won't happen without good records.

Above all, hire a bookkeeper to make sure all your official financial and tax records are tracked correctly. Your bookkeeper will help you keep everything organized and up to date. Keeping solid records of customer data is also important. This could be your client roster, affiliate manager contacts, suppliers, and so on. Having all of this organized makes your business more attractive to buyers.

Systems Are a Must

Buyers are also looking for a business that runs smoothly, efficiently, and with minimal input from the owner. If the business only runs because of you, it's not sellable. That means you need systems and standard operating procedures (SOPs) in place. Automate wherever possible; set up workflows, email sequences, and processes that run without you. If you disappeared tomorrow, could someone else step in and keep the business running?

Document everything you do! Outline exactly how you do everything, from customer service responses to content creation schedules. Buyers love SOPs because, with them, they won't have to figure out everything on their own when you're no longer the owner. If you foresee selling within the year, I recommend outsourcing your current duties now. A business being managed by a team or contractors is more appealing to buyers than one that depends on just one person. If your entire business is built around your personal brand, selling it becomes harder.

Buyers want a business that can continue without the original owner as seamlessly as possible. The more your business depends on systems rather than your presence, the higher its resale value.

Don't Make It Too Personal

Whenever possible, avoid over-personalizing a brand. If the business can only run with your face, name, and presence, it will be harder to sell. If you want real freedom, financial independence, and the option to cash out for life-changing money one day, you need to build with the end in mind. Create something that can thrive without you.

Before launching a new project, product or system, always ask, "Will this make the business easier or harder to sell later?" Even if the idea of selling is years away, act as if you will sell one day. Make decisions now that increase value, not deter it.

Buying vs. Building a Business

If the plan is for your business to be a website, you may be thinking that you will be building a site from scratch. The thing is, it is also possible to buy an established website as your business.

As an entrepreneur who is thinking like a website investor, you get to decide if you will build or buy your business. There are pros and cons to each. The biggest difference is time. Buying an established website allows you to save a significant amount of time. You'd just need to invest more money to acquire it. But don't be discouraged if money is a concern because the great thing here is that there is something for every budget. Starter sites usually cost less than $5,000. More established sites can range from $5,000 to several hundred thousand dollars. As discussed, the price depends on the profit they generate.

So which option is best for you? Well, that really comes down to personal preference and personal budget. If you appreciate saving time and you have the funds to invest, buying an established site will often be the better option. Why? Because an established site already has traffic, subscribers, followers, products, and content. It's active and earning. When you buy a site that is already earning revenue, you start earning your ROI back from day one. Instead of trying to figure out how to build an audience and a product, you can focus on scaling and improving what is currently there.

However, if you are low on funds but have lots of time to spend, buying a starter site may be the right choice for you. Or you may just want to build a website from scratch. Going this "build first" route means you will save money initially; however, the downside is you will spend a lot of time creating a site from the ground up. And you may end up having to spend money to scale it in the long run, anyway. So, you can see why it pays to buy an established site that is already profitable and build from there. When running properly, that's when a site starts printing value like it's your own personal ATM.

Buying a Community

While we are on the topic of buying businesses, it's important to mention another plus. You can buy a business that comes with an active community! Yes, instead of spending years trying to build one from scratch, you can acquire a built-in community in a day. Isn't the future amazing?

When you buy a business with a community, such as an email list, membership or social following, you get to skip the startup phase. Instead of shouting into the void, you acquire a business that's already thriving. It has momentum, active engagement, and, most importantly, paying customers.

Anyone who has launched something from scratch knows the struggle. It's a slow, painful grind to get noticed, build trust, and convert cold leads into buyers. That's why buying a community is the ultimate success jumpstart. It's like fast-forwarding the boring first half of the movie and jumping straight to the part where the main character already has the empire. The main character is you, honey.

The first time I bought a blog that came with a community, I was hooked. The blog acquisition included an email list full of people who were already interested in the niche, already engaged, and already paying attention. This was not my first business acquisition, but it was the first time I inherited an audience that someone else had built.

Until then, I always built my email lists from scratch and spent years growing communities from the ground up. This time, the work had already been done; I was given a pre-warmed, engaged audience on a silver platter. All I had to do was show that audience a great offer. I felt ecstatic.

Black Friday was just around the corner, so I wasted no time in crafting something special for them. Instead of scrambling for new leads, running ads, or begging social media to show my posts to more than five people, I went straight to the source. No fancy launch strategy. No complicated funnel. No endless promotion. Just a simple, well-crafted Black Friday email sequence sent to a list of people who were already paying attention. And it worked.

By the end of the weekend, I had one of my most successful Black Friday sales ever. The kind of numbers that make you wonder why you ever wasted so much time trying to build an audience from scratch. Who knew buying one was this effortless?

That sale event was a wake-up call. It proved something I had already suspected: Community is everything. Anyone can pay for ads to get website traffic. Anyone can get eyeballs on a sales page. But *if a brand has an engaged community, selling can be simple.*

This blog came with a built-in trust factor. The subscribers already knew and liked the brand, so when I introduced an offer that made sense for them, they said, "Heck yes."

That's when I fully understood the power of buying a business with an audience. Instead of spending months (or years) building trust, I got to step in and start making money from day one.

If you are spending all your time trying to build an audience and struggling to gain traction, you might be working harder, not smarter. There is another way. Buying a business that already has an engaged audience is like taking the escalator instead of the stairs. You get to skip the slowest, hardest part and focus on scaling instead of surviving.

That post-acquisition, effortless Black Friday sale was the moment I knew I would never build an audience from scratch again if I could just buy one instead.

Not convinced yet? Here are more reasons why I believe buying a community is worth considering:

Instant Credibility

When you start a new business, you are just some random person on the Internet asking strangers to believe in you. When you buy an existing business with an engaged audience, that trust is already built. People are already following the brand, reading the content, and trusting the recommendations.

Instead of trying to prove yourself, you inherit the credibility that someone else has spent years creating. This means you do not have to:

- Beg for attention because the audience is already there.
- Start from scratch on social media because the followers are already engaged.
- Spend months warming up leads because the brand is already trusted.

Built-In Traffic and Sales From Day One

A business with an existing audience and traffic rolling in is the golden ticket. When people are already coming to the site, engaging with the brand, and buying, more than half of the work is accomplished. All you have to do is optimize, monetize, and scale.

Look at it this way: Would you rather open a restaurant in the middle of nowhere and hope people find it? Or take over a packed, thriving restaurant where the regulars already love the menu?

You Skip the Hardest (And Slowest) Part

Although doable, building from scratch takes time and consistency. Building an audience from the ground up is one of the hardest things you will ever do as a business owner. Growing a social media following and email list can take years, whereas when you acquire a community, you get to skip all of that. Someone else has already done the heavy lifting. Some people grind for years trying to build an audience to sell to. Others buy an existing community and start making money from day one.

It's Easier to Monetize an Engaged Audience

Buying a community means you step into a business that already has buyers, not just followers. This can be a goldmine. When you take over and improve it, you start monetizing faster and have the potential to scale faster by adding new offers to a community that already trusts the brand.

If you have the opportunity to acquire a business that already has a loyal audience, a steady stream of traffic, and a trusted brand, why start one from scratch? Buying a business with a built-in community means you get to skip the slow start-up phase struggle. Smart entrepreneurs don't waste time reinventing the wheel when they can acquire something that is already working.

Either way, your business needs an audience and community. Your success depends on having people who trust your brand enough to open their wallets. So start engaging with your community today. Create, share, connect, and give value. The sales will follow. And before you know it, you will be the person people are looking to for answers.

Website Investing

Now that we've covered the various reasons why I think buying businesses is awesome, let's go a bit deeper. I've done a lot as a creator, but my favorite role is "website investor." As noted previously, it means I buy, grow, and sell websites. As a website investor, you buy a website and then work to boost a site's content, traffic, and revenue. This, in turn, raises its market value. At that point, you can either keep it and enjoy the income it generates or sell it for profit. The reselling side of website investing is often referred to as "website flipping" or "blog flipping."

You probably know about house flipping. That's when someone buys a fixer-upper house, renovates it to boost its value, and then sells it for profit. Well, website flipping is a similar concept. Instead of buying physical real estate, like a house, you buy *digital* real estate, like a website. Flipping websites is cheaper than flipping houses. You don't need a mortgage or a team of construction workers. Running a digital business usually has low costs. Plus, the profit margins can be higher.

I started website flipping in 2018 when I sold my cruelty-free beauty blog for $40,000. I reinvested the money into buying more websites and sold them for profit over the next year. Since then, I have flipped hundreds of websites for myself. I've also been involved in the sale of thousands more as an agent, helping my clients sell their websites. I went from flipping websites on the side to it becoming my full-time career. *Wild!*

Meanwhile, Nick and I renovated and flipped our apartment in Victoria a year after we bought it. The proceeds, plus my website flipping income, bought us our next place, a five-bedroom house. Nick renovated that house, too. We sold it a few years later to buy another five-bedroom house. We have been renovating our current home for a few years. Let me tell you, renovating a house isn't cheap! The cost of lumber and quartz alone is panic-inducing. The costs associated with website flipping, alternatively, are much more manageable.

Some people build or buy websites with the intention of flipping them for profit from the start. While others buy websites to serve a purpose online and then decide to sell them later when they are no longer needed.

When done right, website flipping has the potential to be a lucrative way to make money online. Now, this is not a guarantee. I'm not going to say it will for sure be lucrative for *you*, as there's no way for me to know what your success as a website investor could be. There are too many variables, and I don't know your skills or your work ethic. What I can give you is stats from sales I've experienced personally, as well as successes I've helped my clients achieve.

Over the years, I've bought and sold many websites. For example, I bought a blog in a design niche for $30,000 and sold it for $130,000 three months later. Additionally, during the three months I owned it, the site earned $25,000. So, the total profit of that flip was $125,000. Another time, I bought a self-care niche blog for $6,000, held it for a few months while it earned $1,000 a month, and then flipped it for $36,000. But wait until you hear what kind of results my clients have achieved:

- I coached Alison to develop her self-care site, and she was able to sell it for $35,000.
- Emily sold her food blog for $150,000.
- Beth sold her homeschooling blog for $52,000.
- Chrissy sold her blog for $105,000.
- Kate sold her beauty blog for $200,000.
- Brandon sold his yoga blog for $38,000.
- Kyle sold his reviews site for $325,000.

Each of these clients sold their business on my platform, NicheInvestor.com. Now, while this might sound great, and you may see dollar signs dancing in your mind right now, hold your horses, cowgirl. *Website investing is not a get-rich-quick kind of thing.* It's important to understand that it requires work and dedication to invest in digital businesses, improve them, and get them to the point of being worth something at resale.

However, if you're willing to put in the effort, you might fall in love with website investing like I did. It's a super flexible job you can do from home on your own time, and you get full control over how you want to monetize and grow your site. I like that there is no cap or limit to how much money I can make flipping websites. I am only limited by my own choices in how much time and effort I wish to put into it.

In addition to the income, website flipping is a low-barrier-to-entry way to make money online. Anyone can do it, and you don't need to spend hundreds of thousands to get started. It is an asset you control, unlike the stock market, which goes up and down, out of your control.

With website investing, you are buying a revenue-generating asset that you can improve as you wish and resell when you wish. I love website investing because it offers a great chance to learn high-income skills, too. You will pick up copywriting, SEO, marketing, and web design along the way. If you enjoy blogging and digital marketing, these are skills you could utilize to flip multiple websites a year.

You don't need design or tech skills to buy a website. You just have to know what to look for and be able to learn how to improve it. This way, you can sell it for a higher price. What kind of price? Believe it or not, people are willing to pay top dollar for a great website. To give you an idea of the kind of multiples websites sell for in the market, the industry standard is typically 20-40 times their monthly profits. In other words, if a website earns $1,000 a month and has a good amount of organic traffic, it may sell in the range of $20,000 to $40,000. The better shape your website is in, the higher the price it can go for. So it's well worth spending some time preparing your website for sale in order to get the best price.

Yes, earlier in this book, I told you *not* to overthink your offer and to just get it out into the world already. And I stand by that! Your idea isn't going to sell itself from the safety of your brain. Here's where the nuance kicks in: Speed is for launching, and a well-planned strategy is for scaling. You need both. It's not contradictory to move fast on your first product *and* take your sweet time planning your exit.

In fact, that's how the smartest founders do it. You act now so you can start learning, testing, and earning. You also start setting your business up like an asset that a future buyer will want to own. This means you need to keep good financial records. You should build systems, track your wins, and set up multiple revenue streams. That's how you build with the long game in mind. With one quick action at a time and a long-term vision.

So how do you get started with website investing?

The easiest (read: least chaotic) way to enter the website investing and flipping industry is to snag an already-established site. I'm talking one that's not just sitting there looking pretty, but actually pulling in traffic and revenue. Look for one with content and digital products that already make money. This way you aren't starting at zero. Your job is to improve that content, better monetize it, and grow it further.

Or you could build a site from scratch. There are pros and cons to each. The biggest difference is time. Buying an established website allows you to save a significant amount of time. You'd just need to invest more money to acquire it. But don't be discouraged if money is a concern, because the great thing here is that there is something for every budget. Starter sites usually cost less than $5,000. More established sites can range from $5,000 to several hundred thousand dollars. The price depends on the profit they generate.

So which option is best for you? Well, that really comes down to personal preference and personal budget. If you appreciate saving time and you have the funds to invest, buying an established site will often be the better option. Why? Because an established site already has traffic, subscribers, followers, products, and content. It's active and earning. When you buy a site that is already earning revenue, you start earning your ROI back from day one. Instead of trying to figure out how to build an audience and a product, you can focus on scaling and improving what is currently there.

However, if you are low on funds but have lots of time to spend, buying a starter site may be the right choice for you. Or if you are happy to spend more time than money entirely, then building a website from scratch could be your avenue. Going the 'build first' route means you will save money initially. But the downside is you will spend a lot of time creating a site from the ground up. And you may end up having to spend money to scale it in the long run, to grow it anyway. So you can see why it pays to buy an established site that is already profitable, and build from there.

Have a website to sell?
To find out how much your site is worth, visit HerPaperRoute.com/val where you'll be given a suggested price range and options for selling on our platform.
Looking to buy a website?
Visit HerPaperRoute.com/listings to see what we have available for sale this week.

What to Look for When Buying a Website

When considering making an offer on a website, the first obvious thing to consider is the net profit it generates. Make sure that the monetization streams make sense to you, and consider how you could increase revenue moving forward. Also, look at the expenses and see if you could reduce them. This could be removing unnecessary subscriptions, plugins or other costs, or switching to more affordable alternatives. But beyond financials, there's actually a few less obvious things that, in my opinion, are just as important.

1. Do you understand and enjoy the niche? You don't have to buy a website in a niche you like, but it sure can help. Purchasing a website in a niche that you have very little knowledge of may make the scaling and flipping process more stressful than it needs to be. And you're more than likely going to discover that you don't have any enjoyment from the experience. It's *always* easier to make money and succeed with a website you enjoy working on.

For example, I don't know anything about cars. I don't even drive! So if I were to buy a car niche website, I'd probably tank it and lose money. I'd be bored with the content and wouldn't feel inspired or motivated to put any effort in to work on it.

On the other hand, my uncle who is a mechanic could probably take any car blog and make it pay his mortgage with ease. The difference is one person knows a lot about cars and finds them interesting, the other doesn't. The website is the same either way. Do you see how you are the common denominator in the success of a website?

2. Does it come with a community? Ideally, you want the website to come with an email list and social followers. An active mailing list is a key way to earn money from your website. It can also help protect your site from future search engine algorithm changes.

3. How does the due diligence look? When looking at a website for sale, always ask to be added to the site's Google Analytics. This way, you can see what the traffic history is with your own eyes. Also, review the profit and loss sheet thoroughly.

Check screenshots of payments to confirm that the financial claims are correct. Taking the time to do your due diligence will help ensure that you are purchasing a website that's a good fit for you.

You'll find a copy of my due diligence checklist for free in the bonus materials that come with this book.
Find it at GlowUpYourself.com/bonus

Before you throw your money at a website, let's pump the brakes and get real about one more thing. It's super important to note that something that might make a website perfect for one person might be what makes it wrong for someone else.

What feels like a cakewalk to one person might feel like climbing Everest in Jeffrey Campbell Lita boots to someone else. So no, I can't tell you what'll be "easy" but I can give you this golden rule: Stick to what you know. Buy in niches you understand. Go for monetization models you can either run yourself, or happily hand off to someone who knows what they're doing.

In other words, consider the stuff that looks good on paper, like the metrics, but at the end of the day, don't underestimate the importance of picking a project that will suit your lifestyle.

So, ask yourself, what's the endgame? Are you dreaming of a low-maintenance project that just needs a little design update? Or are you feeling spicy and ready to adopt a full-blown fixer-upper that's going to need love, caffeine, and a six-month growth plan?

Either way is totally valid, but it does boil down to your vibe, your skillset, and how much of your sanity you're willing to employ.

When It's Time To Sell Your Business, Do This

When you're ready to sell your business, use this as your 'business staging cheat sheet.' Just as you'd stage your home before putting it on the market for sale, you want your business to look its best, too. The fact is, your business isn't going to be right for everyone, and you will most likely have to deal with a lot of nos before you find the right buyer. However, there are things you can control and do to give your business the best chance of attracting buyers:

1. **Keep traffic up**. Keep the traffic coming, whether it's organic traffic from social media, Pinterest, search engines, or paid traffic from ads. Or a mix of both. The more people who visit your website, the better.

2. **Keep profit up**. Don't overspend on things that aren't necessary. A business that earns $100,000 but has $90,000 in expenses is worth less than one that makes $50,000 with only $5,000 in expenses.

3. **Keep the newsletter active**. Buyers want to see that your business comes with a community. An email list of subscribers is very valuable. But it can't be a list of cold subscribers who haven't opened an email in months. Keep the list clean and active. Remove cold subscribers,

bring in new subscribers, and send frequent newsletters.

4. **Make every piece of content high quality**. Your blog content, sales pages, and offers are the real MVPs. Quality content establishes your website as a trusted source. It also justifies a higher asking price.

Let me add something about content while we're here. Buyers want more than average when it comes to the content on a site. A buyer's main objective is to buy a website to save time by not having to create a bunch of content themselves. They want to acquire a website with exceptional content that they can scale. They don't want to buy a site where they'd have to do a ton of editing to fix bad content.

Basically, they're looking for amazing content that makes them say, "I couldn't make this myself. Take my money!" If your blog posts seem stale, your sales pages are weak, or your offers lack substance, you're pushing potential buyers away. With great content, buyers will see your site as an exciting investment rather than just another website. Furthermore, great content shows buyers you're trustworthy and reassures them they won't waste their money on a lemon. High-quality content is your power play and is what will make your business stand out in the sea of other listings.

Rejection

Rejection hurts. I won't sugarcoat it. It feels personal. Like a neon sign flashing "YOU SUCK" directly into your soul. It's especially tough when you put your business up for sale in the market. Selling your business is not for the emotionally fragile. You built this thing from the ground up and poured years into creating content, scaling it, tweaking it, and making it profitable. It's your baby. And now, there it is, up for public dissection like a contestant on *Shark Tank*. Being poked, prodded, and questioned by strangers who don't have the same sentimental attachment you do. And that stings.

Most of the time, instead of an instant "We'll take it!" you'll get...rejection, crickets, ghosted. Lowball offers that feel personally offensive. Welcome to the emotional rollercoaster of selling a business! I've helped my clients sell thousands of digital companies over the years, and I've been in the seller's seat many times myself, as well. I've seen it all.

Of course, we want potential buyers to be as in love with our businesses as we are. To see the late nights, the passion, the brilliant vision behind it. Yet 99.9% of the time, buyers don't give a rat's gyat about any of that. They're not there to admire your creative genius. They're there for the cold, hard facts: revenue numbers, traffic stats, and content quality. That's it. They're making a business decision, not an emotional one. And that's a good thing because it means you don't have to charm them; you just have to show them the value.

Yet, the selling process can still take its toll on a seller. This is especially true once offers start coming in. You might think a sale is a sure thing. But then you get an "actually, nah" on the day you planned to enter escrow.

When I had a buyer for Niche Investor, I thought the six-figure deal was in the bag. The paperwork was signed, and escrow was about to open. That day, I ordered my coffee at a Tim Hortons, thinking I was about to enter a new tax bracket. I imagined all the new investments I could make with my pile of cash from the sale. Would I develop one of those choppy, "eh-eh-eh"–sounding laughs that wealthy old men named Wharton have? Then, an email from the buyer appeared, stating that he was backing out at the last minute, the $560,000 sale canceled. Um, can I return this coffee? I'm financially ruined, actually.

Most of the time, people's reasons for not moving forward are entirely reasonable, yet sometimes, the excuse for a no is ridiculous.

"I asked my dog, and he barked twice, which means no in our special communication system." (I would love to see the due diligence checklist that includes "Dog's Opinion" as a key factor.)

"I saw a competitor blogging about a similar product, and I just can't handle that energy." (Do you know how many coffee shops exist worldwide? Relax.)

"I don't trust things I can't physically touch." (Sir, this is a digital business. Would you like me to print out the website and mail it to you?)

As you design your glow-up journey, you'll face many types of rejection. First, breathe! It happens to quite literally everyone who dares to get off the couch and pursue something grander.

A client says no? Cool, maybe you just dodged a nightmare customer who would have drained your energy. An investor isn't interested? Great, now you're free to build something on your terms without their micromanaging. A brand doesn't want to work with you? Their loss, not yours! Because the right brand is out there looking for exactly what you bring to the table. Someone left a nasty comment? It's OK! The ones who have something negative to say will only ever sit in the stands, watching, commenting, but never actually doing anything.

Friend, I'm not going to tell you to stop caring what people think because, let's be real, we're human; we care. What matters is that you stop caring *what the wrong people think*. The keyboard critics who have never built anything in their lives? Not your problem. The family member who doesn't "get" what you're doing and thinks you should get a real job? Not your problem. The trolls who exist purely to project their own insecurity onto you? Again—not your circus, not your monkeys. *Your job is to stay focused on your vision*.

Feel the feelings, but don't let them drive. You're allowed to have a moment when rejection or criticism stings. Just don't unpack and live there. I like to keep receipts of good feedback instead. Any time you get a compliment, a win, or a glowing testimonial, save it. When doubt creeps in, pull those out and remind yourself why you started.

Rejection is not a neon sign flashing, "YOU SUCK," it's actually a neon sign flashing, "Congrats, you're growing!" It's part of the process. The people who never get rejected are the ones who never try. And it's just a plot twist, really. What if that door slamming in your face is just a redirect to something better? What if you can use this as fuel and not a roadblock? What if you focus on celebrating the guts it took to show up, regardless of the results?

We all have a rejection highlight reel ten miles long. Rejection won't stop happening, unfortunately. So, it pays to have thick skin. However, thick skin doesn't mean you don't have feelings. It means knowing what deserves your energy and what is just background noise. What matters is if you can build a rejection-proof mindset to become unbothered by it.

The next time you hear no, say, "Thank you" to the universe. Seriously. Because that no is making room for the much better thing that's coming. Or if you're feeling extra spicy, the next time something doesn't go how you hoped, yell out "REMIX!!!" It's extra fun if you yell it in public.

9

When Everything Goes Wrong

How I Nearly Destroyed My Company

Allow me to regale you with the account of how I nearly destroyed my business and drove it into the ground. Brace yourselves. This is about to be a whole new level of cringe—and a dire cautionary tale.

It starts in 2022. My company was thriving during the first couple of years of the pandemic. We experienced record engagement on our social media. Droves of people were signing up for our programs and purchasing businesses on our investor platform. Ad revenue was up. Blog traffic was up. Email open rates were, you guessed it, up!

For a moment in time, it felt like everyone who was stuck at home was choosing to spend their time on one of my websites, buying things. Everything I launched was a hit. Business was booming! Things were going so well; I was making more money than ever before in my life. That is until I began making a series of mistakes that would threaten to destroy everything.

The first mistake I made was to assume that the numbers would always be that high. I feel silly saying this now, but I really thought the record sales, traffic numbers, and deal flow we had after the pandemic would last forever. This new normal is great. This must be how it feels to be a successful business owner. Now that we've reached this level of success, surely it's only up from here!

Well, *thinking* that wasn't the mistake, but making investments based on that assumption was.

Niche Investor, my website flipping platform, was growing fast and in high demand. Up until that point, I'd been running it all on my own, and I was burning out. I knew it was past time to hire a team to help manage it. Ah, yes, mistake number two.

To clarify, again, hiring help was not a mistake, but hiring too many people too fast was. That year, I hired six employees. This might not sound like much, but for the type of business it was (asynchronous and digital), it was way too many people. The people I hired were wonderful, but —not due to any fault of theirs—I found it incredibly stressful having to manage everyone's needs.

My original intention was to delegate some of my workload so I could focus on other things. Yet, because I had hired too fast, I made way more work for myself. Truthfully, I was overwhelmed by having to answer constant emails from my new employees and provide the support they needed at all times. This is just growing pains; it will get easier, right? *Riiiight?!*

Around this time, there was a lot of messaging going around online about getting to the "next level." For example, "If you're at one million, you need a coach who can take you to ten million!" I was seeing these kinds of sentiments everywhere, in comments, in ads, in emails. NEXT LEVEL. LEVEL UP. SCALE UP. My company was dancing on the one-million-dollar mark. So, I assumed that I should be concerned with pushing it over the line and into multimillion numbers. That's the next natural move, right? *Riiiight?!* I thought I was doing the right thing when I sent $50,000 to a coach to join her group program. It was a hair-raising number, one that I no doubt should not have thrown at a coaching program. But, in that moment, I believed the hype. I believed that this was what you were supposed to do when you were ready to scale up. I bet you can see where this is going...I was wrong.

At the time I enrolled, my self-study digital courses were selling well. Over the years, I'd built up a good, automated funnel for selling them that was generating sales passively. However, the coach advised her students to immediately shut down all of our self-study courses in favor of opening one high-ticket group coaching program similar to hers.

Why did she advise this? She said we should direct all of our clients into one signature program so as not to confuse our clients with too many choices. This felt like a risk to me. My intuition was doing a little cha-cha-cha dance in my head, waving a red flag. I valued my intuition for getting me here, but I wanted to trust the coach's process. Also, I'd just invested so much money into this training. I wanted to follow her instructions to see it through. After all, the other students and I had given her a stack of cash for her high-ticket program, so why wouldn't someone pay us the same if we had our own high-ticket programs?

Ugh. I think this is how people get tricked into cults. Anyway, I can only blame myself for drinking the Kool-Aid. Once inside the program, it became obvious to me that I didn't need to pay a coach $50,000 to tell me to set up a high-ticket coaching program. I already knew how to do and build everything she taught. Most of which I was already operating before enrolling.

Spending a bunch of money on the wrong coach was my mistake. Ignoring my intuition and taking the coach's advice to shut down all my self-study courses was my next mistake. Things got worse.

At this time, Nick and I had completed the renovation of our house and sold it for almost a million dollars, which qualified us for a higher mortgage. Because of how good things were going in my business, we felt like we had a sense of security. Nick's YouTube channel was monetized and starting to grow, too. So when we fell in love with a home that was nearly two million dollars, we thought, we can manage this, right? *Riiiight?!* (Can anyone else hear that *cha-cha-cha* beat playing in the distance?)

Following the coach's instruction, I launched a high-ticket program, although I refused to charge $50,000 for it. That price was NOT something I wanted to charge my clients. I will always remember when I was a struggling new mom and new entrepreneur with no budget who just needed advice. I vowed to make my coaching programs accessible for this reason. I priced my new program at only slightly more than what my self-study courses cost, with enough of an increase that I could provide the level of value and support to make it possible. And to my surprise, it started selling right away! I was enrolling high-ticket clients. *Hooray!*

What I didn't realize yet, though, was that the cost of shutting down my self-study programs was substantial. By closing those more affordable courses, I had effectively shut off the tap to a whole audience as well as a funnel that had been a significant lead magnet for my company. Still, money was flowing in, and things *felt* like they were ramping up, so I continued to wonder, what's next?

Other companies like mine were sponsoring events and booths at conferences and trade shows. Should I do that, too? I signed for a $10,000 one here, a $15,000 one there. Over the next two years, I traveled the continent. I hosted events, spoke on stages, and networked at conferences. This expense will pay off, right? *Riiiight?!*

And I saw other entrepreneurs appearing on popular podcasts and morning shows on TV. Should I be doing that, too? What would a businessperson do to get more publicity? Hire a publicist, of course! So that's what I did. I signed off on another $20,000 to pay a publicist, thinking it would be the ticket to launch my name into the stars. I'd become a household name, I'd appear on all the hottest talk shows and best podcasts, and everyone would want to work with us. Fame is the next level to aspire to, right? *Riiiight?! Cha-cha-cha.*

As I stood at the gate, ready to board the plane home from another conference, disappointment washed over me. Looking at the numbers from the event, I'd only collected 150 email subscribers. After a full three days of canvassing! The number was dismal, considering 10,000 attendees had been there, and I'd paid roughly $12,000 for the booth. Lame.

A text popped up from someone on my team, her third message that weekend, "Meghan is getting all the listings! Why can't I get any? Why is it so slow right now?"

Annoyed, I wanted to remind her that her job is to go out on the Internet to *find* sellers to list, not wait for me to assign listings to her. And that her coworker Meghan was getting listings because she was actively networking with website owners and signing them. Sure, she had every right to be concerned about the state of the industry, but I was not the right person to complain about that to, so her text irritated me.

I was feeling the pressure from every angle, and I did not need to hear any of that right then. Regardless, I chose to bite my tongue and reply with a softer, less hostile response. "I feel you! How about we meet over Zoom on Monday to brainstorm some ideas you can use to network with more potential sellers?"

The state of the industry was weighing on us all. Not to mention, I'd been working with my publicist for several months, and they hadn't delivered on their promise to book me on any top podcasts or TV shows. *Bummer*.

At least my high-ticket program was going well. I was fueled by the positive results I was bringing to my clients, but unfortunately, I was still burned out. Even more so than before. Having to give so much of my time and energy to my many new high-ticket clients was draining me. I had to pull back from my other duties, so I started outsourcing the job of writing blog posts and social media content.

Soon, I became less and less involved in my own company. Creating content was my favorite part of the job, but now it was like my voice wasn't in the brand anymore. I had removed myself too far from the business. The soul of the company was missing.

By now, the novelty of living in a $2 million dream home had worn off. I was dealing with the painful reality of the hefty mortgage payments and property taxes. House expenses were costing me about $80,000 a year! And that's not even counting bills or groceries! Let me tell you, I longed for a smaller house daily. Remember how I used to pay a couple hundred bucks a month to live in Kylie's closet in Hollywood? Things were so simple back then.

Over at Niche Investor, my team was handling things efficiently, but I was still struggling to enjoy managing them. I missed the days when I was a solopreneur, when I could work on my creative projects uninterrupted.

As I stepped onto the plane and found my seat, another message popped up from someone on my team needing something from me again. Just figure it out yourselves! I wanted to scream. I should be relaxing and enjoying this flight, but I was dreading having to even think about my stupid business. The thought of having to look at even one more email filled me with agony.

Reality sank in; I resented the company I'd built. I was in way over my head and totally burned out. I had committed myself to paying for too many expenses, had. Flown too close to the sun. I was in too deep.

Just then, the next song started playing in my earbuds, Sum 41's "In Too Deep." Ha, how fitting! I thought as I recalled dancing on the tables to this soon as a teenager, in the back room of my bakery job. Back when feeling in too deep was due to not much more than having too much homework. The song had a whole new meaning for me just then. I slumped my head into my hands in dismay. What am I going to do?

A scary feeling of dread attached itself to me in 2023. So, for a while, I was making decisions from a place of anxiety and desperation rather than love and abundance. Ultimately, it was my company that would suffer the consequences. It certainly didn't help that, by the summer of 2023, pandemic lockdowns were lifted, and most people returned to their offices. Which meant fewer people were online, buying things from websites.

We started to see sales slow down. Industry ad revenue RPM rates started to dip. Stocks I'd invested in began to decline. As months passed, whispers of a global recession began making headlines. This is OK, I told myself. Things will level out.

Oh, but in September of 2023, all shit hit the fan. A certain search engine made a series of algorithm changes that caused absolute havoc in the content marketing industry. This algorithm change caused many websites to disappear from search pages. As you might imagine, this was very bad. *Catastrophic*, in fact. It decimated the organic traffic and livelihoods of countless website owners. The Internet as we knew it was no more.

Overnight, hundreds of thousands of websites dropped in value, some to almost nothing. Making them worth a fraction of what they once were at resale. No, not all websites, only the ones that relied heavily on that particular search engine. The websites that had diversified their traffic sources, such as the ones that got traffic from Pinterest, were OK.

Fortunately, my sites were built mainly for Pinterest traffic. So, this change didn't affect my niche sites as much. But it did affect Niche Investor because many of the websites we were brokering, i.e., listed for sale, were affected. Sales on the platform slowed to a halt as buyers became scared to invest their money into websites whose traffic had dropped so much. Understandably. Our team scrambled to revalue all our listings. We had to give our clients the unfortunate news that their businesses were no longer worth their previous asking prices.

Thankfully, our listings for websites that had Pinterest traffic were in high demand. Those listings flew off the digital shelves, and we could barely sign new listings like those fast enough. Still, not every buyer knew the value of Pinterest traffic back then. Many older website investors at the time had old-school preferences when it came to SEO. They thought that traditional search engines were the only way to go and didn't understand what Pinterest SEO was.

So there was this divide. On the one hand, we were staying afloat for now, but revenue overall had taken a major hit, and the future of the industry as we knew it was looking grim. I would reassure myself constantly, This is temporary. The industry shift will recover. Everything's going to bounce back. The value of websites will go back up.

Even so, as I sat down to do payroll each month, I'd have a full-on panic attack looking at the numbers. We simply could not afford to keep paying the team with those declining sales. I knew I needed to let some of my team members go. But the thought of having to fire anyone made my skin crawl. I didn't want to hurt anyone. I didn't want to have those tough conversations. *They would hate me!*

So, instead of making any cuts to the team, I decided to first cut back on other expenses—starting with decreasing my own salary. I canceled or scaled back on as many expenses as I could starting with software, advertising, coaches, PR, event sponsorship, and travel. After I cut my salary in order to be able to keep my team employed, I ran the business as leanly as possible for the rest of the year. Yet, their salaries were still one of the biggest expenses I faced, month after month. We needed to make cuts. But I kept thinking, *I don't want to upset anyone!*

Then I got another idea. What if I were to sell Niche Investor? Then I'd be free from this misery, and I wouldn't have to fire anyone. The new owner could simply inherit the team. Brilliant! If only it were that easy. For months, I tried to sell it. Although I came very close with that $560,000 offer, I never found the right buyer to close the deal.

It turns out that trying to sell your business while experiencing active burnout is not a good mix. Giving off "I hate my business, but please, please buy it" energy is not exactly attractive to potential buyers.

Every time I would have to make payroll, I'd have my monthly panic attack. Crying a bit as I sent out everyone's paychecks. They had no idea. I had to pull money from business savings and tax savings for the year to cover the team's salaries. By March of 2024, I couldn't do it anymore. Something had to change, or it was all going to be over.

10

Fixing a Failing Business: Emergency Rescue Plan

Had refunds been a possibility, I would not have gone to the retreat in Mexico that spring. I'd purchased the event ticket over a year earlier when my business was thriving and my industry was booming. The trip was nonrefundable. So there I was, in Puerto Morelos, in a room with a hundred people, who were all seven, eight, and nine-figure CEOs.

I didn't want to be there. Not because I couldn't enjoy the all-inclusive bar (I was fully sober by this time) but because I felt I did not deserve a seat in that room anymore. Now that Niche Investor wasn't at the heights it had once been, who was I to be at a CEO retreat like this?

My other niche sites were experiencing record traffic highs, and my newsletters were growing. Still, I was all consumed with dread about the future of Niche Investor. Everyone here knew me as the founder of what was supposed to be a cool, exciting website-investing startup. I'd attended events a couple of times before with these same people—successful business owners, most of whom were running much larger enterprises. Yet I had always felt confident that I belonged among them. That was until now. My confidence as a CEO and confidence in the investor platform I'd built had taken a nosedive. My dismal perspective now was,"Let me just get this retreat over with and try not to embarrass myself in front of my peers."

Then something spectacular happened. As I started chatting with people, I discovered that *everyone* was feeling the effects of the unstable economy on their industries. Each person I spoke to expressed that it had been a considerably rough year for their company; sales were down all around. It shocked me to learn that these business owners, even the eight-figure ones, were feeling the same types of pressure as I was.

Many people I talked to said they had lost millions in the past year. They blamed factors like the weak economy, rising costs, sluggish consumer spending, and that major search engine change. Interestingly, many also said that they felt they had outsourced too much. They regretted removing themselves so far from their businesses. And they had lost touch with what they had founded. Many admitted they did so when things were going well mid-pandemic. *Sounds familiar!*

"I'm working hard to get myself back into the weeds of my company," one person admitted to me while we sat on the patio by the ocean. "I'm really trying to muscle up the hustle and drive I once had when I was building it as a startup years ago. I realize now that I outsourced too many of the things I enjoyed doing.

I don't feel like it's even my company anymore. So, I'm putting myself back into the daily grind, working to get sales back up, at least to keep the company afloat until the economy picks up."

Hard agree. I'll never forget sitting at that retreat, surrounded by startup founders and CEOs whose companies had more moving parts than a NASA launch. They were brilliant, powerful, deeply accomplished...and completely tangled in red tape. Their stories were full of investor pressure, shareholder drama, bloated payrolls, and decision-making bottlenecks that could derail a pivot before it even got pitched. Worst of all, they had relied so heavily on traditional SEO and that one search engine that they didn't have any other traffic sources in play to fall back on.

And here I was. A digital creator with zero shareholder obligations and no one breathing down my neck about KPIs or profit margins. I wasn't stuck in boardroom purgatory waiting for approval to make a move. *I was the approval.* It dawned on me that I was in a much better position than many of my colleagues. My ability to run a remote business as a solopreneur was my superpower.

While those big businesses scrambled to restructure, downsize, and explain the revenue decline and traffic loss chaos to their stakeholders, it would be no problem for me to quietly assess, pivot, and implement in a matter of days. I could shift strategy without explaining it to anyone. I could rebuild in real time. And most importantly, I could do it on my terms.

That was the moment I stopped seeing my solopreneurship as small and started seeing it as mighty. My lean, flexible business wasn't a liability; it was the solution. While the giants were recalculating, I could be three steps into my next evolution. That's the beauty of building something nimble, focused, and rooted in self-trust. The world will throw a plot twist, and you don't have to crumble. You adapt, pivot, and cash in.

Sometimes, I feel out of place when I talk to CEOs who have achieved more growth than I have. I felt like, What do I even have to offer this person that's of any use to them? and considered staying quiet. Yet, at this retreat, I was taken aback to discover how engaged people were in talking to me. They even asked for my thoughts and advice. *Petit moi*?

That sort of unpretentious openness had a great impact on me. I opened up and shared that my traffic was booming. It came from sources not tied to "The Search Engine." Soon, word spread at the retreat that I was a "Pinterest Queen." People were eager to learn how I managed to grow my organic website traffic to such high numbers without relying on traditional SEO. I was happy to chat all about Pinterest SEO and newsletter list building with everyone.

I learned at the retreat that successful people admit when they don't know something. They also ask for help to learn. They don't try to pretend to know something in an attempt to look smart. They make an effort to *become knowledgeable* about what they aren't familiar with by asking. They view every interaction with others, no matter their level of success, as a chance to learn and grow. Successful people know they don't know it all and that everyone can teach them something.

The biggest lesson I needed came to me on the last day of the retreat. A group had gathered around the pool to chat. I expressed my uncomfortable feelings about having to fire team members, especially ones who have done nothing wrong. But the cost of keeping them on was just too much.

"Been there!" one person declared, "Seriously, don't wait to fire a team member whom you'd be relieved to see go! Even if they are a great employee. Even if they're your friend, if the expense outweighs the benefit, make the call."

Another person added, "The relief you will feel afterward will be well worth the momentary discomfort."

As I looked around the circle, many people were nodding their heads in agreement. "I regret having waited too long to make team cuts," another person sighed, "Hire slow, fire fast!" *Oh, that's a good one.*

On paper, I had done almost everything "right" with Niche Investor. Built systems. Outsourced to a team. Had funnels and opt-ins and automations. But, I had hired way too fast and built a business that no longer felt like me. I had outsourced too far and created a job I didn't want to go to anymore. And the worst part was still trying to keep it all going. Out of guilt. Out of obligation. Out of the desperate hope that one more tweak, one more strategy, one more big client would fix it.

Looking out at the ocean, a feeling of strength washed over me. I got us into this mess, and it was my responsibility to pull us out. I turned back to the group and said the most powerful thing a founder can say: "This isn't working."

It was time to make some big changes and give my business the glow-up it desperately needed before it was too late. By the time I flew home, I knew exactly what I had to do.

Business Glow-Up: How to Fix a Failing Business

If your business feels like it's stalling, it's not a sign to quit. It's a sign to pivot. To strip it down, refocus, and give it a second chance to be the smarter, leaner business that's more aligned with the life you actually want. A business glow-up, if you will.

Once I admitted that Niche Investor was broken, I had to face the reality of why. One of the hardest truths about fixing a failing business is that the systems, subscriptions, or people you thought were crucial may actually be dragging you down. Why not create Glow-Up Quadrants for my business? It worked for my life at thirty. Why wouldn't it work now, for my business at thirty-eight? So, I sat down and created a business Glow-Up Plan for how I was going to turn my ship around. Here's what I did next to correct course and rebuild.

1. I scaled way back. It was clear that the business had a bloated team it didn't need. People were being paid to do work I no longer needed or even wanted them to do, and the overhead was pulling me under.

I made the terrifying decision to let them go (except for one amazing virtual assistant). It was not easy, but I had to make that very necessary hard call. It sucked; It felt awful to have to do it and awful to tell them. Once it was over, I also felt a huge weight disappear almost immediately.

What's that? *Relief?* When the next payroll day came around, incredibly, I didn't have a panic attack this time. I felt empowered by the new structure, just me, my creative brain, and one badass assistant. Before I knew it, I started to feel my confidence coming back. *I can do this.* I can save my company and turn things around!

I also did a major expense audit. What tools was I paying for that I barely used? What recurring expenses could I pause or cancel? What tasks was I outsourcing that could be streamlined, systematized, or delayed? What "nice to haves" are secretly "budget bleeders"? In my business Glow-Up Plan, I made the decision to cut out anything that didn't directly benefit my business. I axed everything that wasn't either making money or making life easier. Offers that drained me, gone. Fancy software and tools I didn't need, canceled.

2. I got real about what Niche Investor actually needed. Why had valuations gone down? Why were people not buying websites like they used to? When I looked at what was working with my other company, HerPaperRoute, it became so obvious what needed to happen at Niche Investor.

HerPaperRoute and my other niche sites were thriving. Their traffic was hitting the highest numbers in years, and their ad revenues were increasing month after month. Why were my sites doing well while other sites weren't? Because none of my own websites relied on traditional SEO or traffic from The Search Engine that everyone else was stressing about. I had traffic because I had content ranking in Pinterest search results, yes. But more importantly, I'd built my own platform via my newsletter. The newsletter gave me 24/7 access to people's inboxes, regardless of what any social media app's algorithm decides to do.

Of course! It was clear to me. I simply needed to educate the buyers and sellers at Niche Investor about Pinterest SEO and the importance of having a newsletter. If both sides of my client base understood this, their websites would thrive. Then, Niche Investor's deal flow and sales would have no choice but to recover. I got to work creating an ebook to train my clients on how to capitalize on Pinterest, and build an email list, and I gave it away for free.

3. I set boundaries. No more scattered energy. No more over-committing myself. I started saying "no thank you" to projects, partnerships, and anything that I didn't feel aligned with. I chose to stop feeling guilty for not being able to reply to every single text. At the same time, I ensured that I made time to show up and be there for my friends and family with dedicated in-person hangouts.

Business-wise, I set boundaries by establishing themed work days. This meant certain days were dedicated to content creation, others to general administrative duties, or simply to being a CEO so I could focus on specific goals with no distractions. Then I made, "Don't Bother Chelsea Fridays," where I blocked out my calendar every Friday for all eternity so that no one could book me for meetings that day. Together, this gave my brain space to actually think. Try it!

4. I got back to my zone of genius. Instead of forcing myself to do the things I hated, I focused on what I'm actually good at. Content creation, product development, and building genuine connections with my audience.

Most importantly, I promised myself that from then on, I'd trust my intuition. No more costly coaching programs. Never again will I follow advice that feels wrong. No more trying to scale too fast. Instead, I would choose to focus on getting back to participating in the parts of my business that I loved and missed. What's that? *Blogging*, my friend! I started writing blog content again and brought back the personal touch of my brand.

Well, I'm happy to say that it all paid off. A year after the retreat, Niche Investor was back in the green. Sales recovered. My niche sites were earning more revenue than ever before thanks to prioritizing blogging again. (Thankfully, the industry had bounced back, eventually, too.) As I looked at the end-of-the-month financials after that year, I was floored to discover that Niche Investor had earned its biggest month's profit. My neck hurt from whiplash, but I was, and am, so grateful. Also, by learning to set healthy boundaries, I overcame my burnout.

The same way I suggested that you list some positive actions for each Glow-Up Quadrant in chapter 4, here are some actions I recommend for your business glow-up:

1. **Audit your offers**. Which products are still aligned with your vision? Which ones actually sell? Cut anything that feels heavy, outdated, or confusing.

2. **Cut expenses and anything that drains you**. Tools you haven't used in months? Gone. Commitments that suck your energy? Gone. People that make you cringe every time you think about them? Boy, bye.

3. **Pick one traffic driver**. Don't try to be everywhere. Pick one traffic source (Pinterest, TikTok, or your newsletter) and go vertical on it.

4. **Rebuild your habits**. Recommit to your morning rou-

tine, your time blocks for writing, and your creative work.

Protecting Your Peace

Sometimes, glow-ups look like hiring a dream team and leasing a big fancy office. Other times, they look like firing an entire team, canceling half your software stack, and realizing the real dream was in having both peace and profits all along.

When my business hit the skids, I realized I didn't want to be the CEO of a company that stressed me out 24/7. I didn't want messages and phone calls at all hours, team meetings I dreaded, or the pressure of having to hit sales targets just to make payroll. So, I leaned into solopreneurship intentionally.

Through this experience, I learned that it's okay to scale back. In fact, it is what I need to be happy as an entrepreneur. Scaling back doesn't mean you've failed. It means you're being strategic. It means you're protecting your profit margin, your mental health, and your creative bandwidth.

I know now that I don't like managing a team. I don't like having tons of people in my head, relying on me or doing things for me. You'll often hear people say that you should work "on" your business and not "in" your business. There is nothing wrong with that advice, but, I disagree. Genuinely, I like working "in" my business and doing most of the tasks myself. I actually love operating a solopreneur show. Most of the tedious tasks are handled by AI, while I get to do all the fun stuff that I like doing.

Not having to manage or be responsible for a team of humans is incredibly freeing, both financially and from a mental health perspective. My business thrives when I'm having fun. So, allowing myself to follow the fun has become my ultimate business strategy.

At some point, as business owners, we've all held onto a team member longer than we should have. But having that uncomfortable conversation is crucial. Ask yourself, will you feel relief when they are gone? If yes, don't wait another moment. There's nothing like a crisis to show you what you're made of. I didn't know I could rebuild and better my business until I had to. The more I took action, the louder my self-trust became.

These revelations have shown me that I can shed the identity of what I thought being a CEO was supposed to look like. You can absolutely be a CEO from your couch, without a big team, without a big office, without any flashy accolades. I now know firsthand that scaling too fast is no fun and that slow growth is awesome. The biggest takeaway here is to listen to your intuition, scale slowly, and let go of the pressure to grow faster than feels right. Follow the fun instead.

If your business has felt messy, too expensive, too chaotic, and too "not you," then take this chapter as your sign to evolve it. In life and in business, glow-ups happen when you stop pretending everything is fine and start making the shifts you've been avoiding. Strip it down, clean it up, and rebuild the business that actually fits your life now. No more clinging to offers you resent, tools you don't use, or strategies that worked for someone else's audience.

This is your reinvention era, which means everything, including your business, should feel aligned, streamlined, and abundant. You don't have to scrap everything to glow up your business. You just have to be bold enough to let go of what's no longer working, honest enough to simplify, and confident enough to bet on yourself again.

11

Looking the Part

Up until now, I've emphasized your internal glow-up (mindset shifts and new habits) and your financial glow-up (how to take action today and build a business) all things to level up your life. Now, if you have been patiently waiting for the part where we talk about your *external* glow-up, welcome. You have arrived. You deserve a style glow-up, too.

Like it or not, appearances matter. Yes, it's a luxury to have the freedom to work from home in our pj's, and I will always value my cozy homebody attire! Yet, when I show up for my client on a coaching call or step out to the grocery store, I'm going to dress well.

Tip Ratio

Looking your best is not about impressing others or fitting into some impossible beauty standard. To me, it is about showing respect for yourself and your clients in a way that makes you feel confident. Because when you look put together, you feel put together.

And when you feel put together, you start moving through life in your highest form.

This lesson smacked me in the face when I was a young university student and waitress. I was assisting my manager at the restaurant with some admin work in the office behind the kitchen. We were tallying tip-out percentages for the line cooks when I was handed a list of numbers. It was a record of each server's nightly tip amounts from the past month.

My task was to check the numbers and make sure each cook and dishwasher received their fair share of the servers' tips each night. I skimmed the amounts, noting that everything looked normal. Out of curiosity, I had to see how my tips compared to my coworkers' (you'd be curious too, don't play!).

Beside each server's name was their nightly sales number, nightly tip amount, and their tip-to-sales percentage. I skimmed the line of names. Alright, my tip amounts were on par with pretty much every other server. But then, BOOM. Valerie.

Valerie's tip-to-sales percentage was astronomically high. She was making way more money than I was. A *lot* more. To my surprise, Miss V was making significantly higher tips than any other girl, *night after night.*

Well, that was all the proof I needed. I now had fiscal proof that being conventionally hot came with financial benefits. You see, Valerie was blonde, tan, curvy, and attractive in an Abercrombie way. The epitome of a beige cardigan on an off-duty Playboy model. That style wasn't my thing. My style at the time was more indie-hipster art school chick. But I had bills to pay, so it was time I learned how to cosplay as a hot person.

From that moment on, I made a mental note of all things Valerie (not in an obsessive, "I want to be you" kind of way, more like in a "I need some style inspo for the purpose of positioning myself as a more conventionally attractive waitress" kind of way): How she carried herself, shoulders back, good posture; how she did her makeup and hair, pretty and tidy; how she spoke. So classy!

More importantly, I observed how she interacted with customers. She spoke to them with assertiveness while giving off a very relaxed, laid-back energy. She came across as cool and aloof with her customers. Not goofy and hyper like I did. Your energy is the first impression you give people. The way you walk into a room, the way you hold yourself, the way you speak with conviction; it all matters.

I even noticed how she held her phone when she texted. It was so ladylike. One dainty index finger lightly tap-tapping at the screen while her other hand gently held the phone. Not to be confused with my texting, which was a chaotic, two-thumbs-going-a-million-miles-a-minute style.

So, I started doing my hair in a more flattering way. I improved my makeup. I started speaking with more confidence. Was it shallow to try to make myself look a certain way at work to get more tips? You bet! Is that how the world works? Absolutely.

All this might sound very dumb to you, but honestly, this research was worth it. Yes, my tips increased. Instant pay-off! However, something bigger happened.

What started as a way to make myself appear cooler and hotter on the floor of the restaurant ended up being valuable life and social skills.

Mindset exercise: Pretend that everyone is in love with you. Not in an arrogant way, but just in your mind, secretly. Imagine that literally everyone you meet has the biggest crush on you! The delivery person, the Uber driver, the gatekeeper of the stage you want to speak on, the investors you want to buy your company. Everyone!

How differently would you move through the world if you pretended everyone was in love with you? You'd probably be kinder, have more patience, and radiate at a more loving frequency, yourself. You'd get into a high vibration pretty fast, I bet. Allowing you to manifest at record speed, and you'd probably have more fun!

Dress for the Role You Want

By emulating the classy traits I saw in Valerie, I was training myself to carry myself with more respect. I wasn't trying to be Valerie; rather, I was using her way of being as a training manual to help bring out my better, most polished self. I learned how to look my best and control a room with quiet confidence, raising my social currency. All of which still comes in super handy, years later.

Take a look at your wardrobe and be honest; could you stand to dress a bit better? A bit more professional? What's going on with your hair right now? It might be time to upgrade your style, hair, and makeup. We all want a polished and intentional aesthetic on the outside that matches how good we feel on the inside, right?

Dressing in a more professional manner doesn't mean losing your unique style. It can simply mean dressing in clothes made of better-quality fabrics and colors that suit you better. It really helps to know what your color season is so you can dress in the colors that look best on you. Look up "color analysis seasons" on your favorite search engine to figure it out. When you know what colors suit you, things like makeup, hair, and clothing become easy.

Hot tip to discover the colors that suit you best:
What celebrity do people say you look like? Find a celebrity with a similar eye, skin, and hair color to you, and study what clothing and hair colors and styles look best on them. Your celebrity look-alike pays a lot of money to their stylist to keep them in their most attractive colors. You can benefit from this for free by using their best looks as your guide!

Nowadays, I have figured out a style of my own, along with a skincare and hair routine that works for me. Your personal style can be anything you want it to be, and your beauty routine can be as low- or high-maintenance as you'd like. So long as you feel good about it. That's all that matters.

Here's a cheat sheet with my external glow-up list, which you might also want to consider for yours, in no particular order:

- Drinking a lot of water and eating vegetables.

- Having a capsule wardrobe.
- Korean skincare.
- Walking more than I sit.
- Red light therapy lamps.
- Meditation.
- Hydrafacials.
- Teeth whitening.
- Knowing my color "season."
- Hair oil.
- Sunscreen every day.

When you look good, you send a message to the world that you value and prioritize yourself. Yes. Mindset matters. Financial growth matters. But don't underestimate the power of showing up looking hot. However, you define hot to be.

17 Things I Stopped Doing to Uncover My Best Self

Many things society views as normal are actually super harmful to your health, mindset, and success. Reflecting on my twenties, I now see how I exposed myself to many low-vibration influences that weighed me down. As they say, hindsight is rose-tinted lemonade...or something like that.

That's why when I finally released the bad stuff from my orbit, it opened up space for good things to surround me. When you do this, your life has no choice but to improve. Toxic friendships, negative self-talk, low-vibe habits—out the door they go. *Don't let the door hit ya where your maker split ya!*

Once I began removing what held me back, my glow-up became inevitable. And yours will be, too. Maybe you're wondering where to even start. Allow me to share some of the things I stopped doing to help usher in my best self. Of course, everyone's goals and situations are different. What I let go of may not be what someone else needs to release. Take what resonates with you, and leave the rest. If this list helps you, great!

These are the biggest negative energies I cut out of my life while designing my glow-up.

1. Drinking alcohol. Alcohol is a toxin. It offers no health benefits. Yet, it takes so much away from your life, health, relationships, and even your beauty. It also lowers your moral compass and makes you more susceptible to saying yes to other lousy vices. Letting go of a drinking habit is one of the best things you can do for yourself.

As I write this, it's been ten years since the last time I was drunk. Ten whole years! That's how many seasons we watched of *Vanderpump Rules* before we were introduced to Scandoval. If you've been a party girl or relate to the VPR cast, you'll get why this analogy fits. Nowadays, I might have a glass of wine once in a blue moon, but never enough to get tipsy and start howling at it.

How did I cut out alcohol? Flip back to chapter 4, where we explored the importance of identity as it relates to habits and goals because what's there is exactly how. I took on the identity of the person I wanted to be by openly stating things like, "I don't like alcohol" and "I'm not a drinker." Before long, my brain believed it, so it became true, and it stuck.

2. Saying yes to things I don't want to do. Boundaries, baby! You need them! If you are prone to people-pleasing, stop yourself and exercise your ability to say no! Setting healthy boundaries for yourself and how you spend your energy is huge. What if the next time someone asks you to do something you don't want to do, you say, "No, thank you," without further explanation? It'd be kinda badass, honestly.

As a chronic people-pleaser, I eventually learned to stand up for myself and say no to doing anything unless I was a) being paid royally for it or b) really wanted to do it. Try saying no. You'll love it. And people will respect you for it.

3. Eating crappy food. There was a time when I could only eat whatever I could afford to get. There was also a time when I lined up for the food bank and was grateful for what was available. I did not have the luxury of being picky. Even then, I knew that eating healthy does not have to mean expensive. Maybe I couldn't buy the organic avocados, but I would still eat healthy.

Choosing to avoid fast food was easy. Riding the bus to smaller mom-and-pop grocery stores was a little inconvenient, but it helped me shop smarter. Nowadays, I do have the luxury of being picky, and I choose to spend my money on organic groceries as much as I can.

A vegetarian diet might not suit everyone, but it has worked well for me. If you're curious, I strongly suggest you give it a try. Also, when you eat organic and plant-based foods, you feel good. Your impact on the planet and harm to animals is lighter, too.

I know you're thinking, yeah, but isn't organic food more expensive? In some places, yes. I remind myself why it's worth it by remembering this quote by organic food advocate Birke Baehr:

> *"When it comes to buying organic food or not, you can either pay for it at the grocery store now, or you can pay for it later at the hospital."*

4. Looking at a scale. Free yourself from the scale. Get rid of it. You will love the freedom you will feel when you no longer check your weight. Just eat healthy, move every day, and appreciate yourself.

5. Consuming dairy. No other animal drinks milk past infancy, especially the milk of another species. So why do humans drink cow's milk? It's very weird. I stopped drinking milk many years ago. If you asked me, organic almond milk is far superior.

6. Following fashion trends. As a kid, I loved fashion magazines. I often tried to copy the models' outfits using thrift store finds. Later, as an adult, I realized just how silly it is to allow trends to dictate what you wear. Plus, not every trend looks good on everyone. It's more important to just wear what feels right to you.

7. Sitting all day. Running a company from home allows me the privilege of working in bed snuggled up with my dog. Since

I'm a homebody who loves coziness, this is perfect for me. The problem is that it's also too easy to get in the habit of not exercising, which, of course, is detrimental. I solved this when I purchased a home treadmill. Now I spend at least fifteen minutes jogging or power walking on it each day while I do social media tasks or writing. Easy.

8. Comparing myself to others. It's oh so easy to fall into the trap of comparing yourself to others these days, especially on social media where you only ever see the perfect highlight reels. I try not to compare myself to others. I put my energy into my own growth instead.

9. Seeking outside validation. If you expect validation from others, girl, you will be very disappointed. People have their own lives, and most people don't care about what anyone else has going on. Learn to validate yourself.

10. Dwelling on the past. The past doesn't exist. Repeat that! What happened before is done and gone and only feels real because it's in your memory. But it's not real. The only thing that is real is the present moment you are in. Focus on your present moment and enjoy every second.

11. Hanging out with low-vibe people. When you cut out negative influences and spend time with positive people, your world expands. So, the toxic people in your life have to go. Instead, focus on building strong relationships with positive, success-driven, and healthy individuals.

12. Overthinking. Stop overthinking things you can't control, and learn to trust your intuition. Your intuition has your best possible outcome at heart.

13. Holding grudges. Learn to practice forgiveness. Accept that people make mistakes and that some people are simply jerks. Forgiving people doesn't mean you accept their bad behavior; it just means their actions don't stick to you. You are above that; you are at peace, healed, and have moved on.

14. Dwelling on failures or rejection. A failure is nothing more than a stepping stone in your path to success. Focus on the lessons learned from experiences of failure or rejection. Be grateful for the chance they give you to try and grow from them. On your journey to success, the universe may test you. These challenges prepare you for your big break.

15. Negative self-talk. One of the most important ingredients you need in your self-improvement journey is to let go of speaking to yourself negatively and to cultivate a positive mindset. How? By practicing positive self-talk. That means saying nice things about yourself to yourself all the time. Anytime you walk by a mirror, stop and say, "Wow, hottie!" regardless of how you're dressed or if you're wearing makeup or not. Eliminate negative self-talk from your vocabulary.

16. Worrying about things I can't control. If you can't change it, don't waste your energy worrying about it. Focus on what you can control.

17. Seeking perfection. As discussed numerous times throughout this book, waiting for perfection blocks action. Many people struggle to take action. They worry too much about making everything perfect. Stop holding yourself back! Don't let the fear of not being good enough stop you from starting a business, writing a book, or improving yourself. Perfection comes from practice, experience, and trial and error.

How do you think you will ever get that experience if you never begin and practice? Again, done is better than perfect. Focus on progress, not perfection. Let your skills grow and get better with time. What negative things will you cut out of your life today?

Your Celebrity Rebrand Plan (For When You've Been a PR Nightmare)

We've discussed how to turn your business idea into reality and how to handle "failure." Now, this is the perfect time for a quick exercise to address another challenge. What happens if you find yourself in a public scandal? What if you or your business gets "canceled"?

I know this is not fun to think about. A public scandal might not happen to you, but it's wise to have a PR action plan just in case things go wrong. From a public relations perspective, I believe every business owner should have a game plan for a potential PR crisis. Planning ahead means you won't have to scramble, fumble, and panic during times of turmoil.

Let's pretend that you are a celebrity or some other type of high-profile individual. You might already be a celebrity. If you are, no need to pretend! Also, please mention how much you love this book on your next late-night talk show. Thanks, girl! Love you!

But for the rest of us non-celebs, it's time to pretend. Imagine you've done something to hurt your public image. Now, you've been "canceled" and you're facing backlash from fans and critics. So you've hired a PR agent for PR crisis intervention in the hopes of cleaning up your image. In this scenario, I'll play your PR agent.

My duty is clear: change how people see you, fix your reputation, rebuild trust in your brand, and discover new business opportunities for you. It can take a long time to transform public perception and repair brand credibility, but here's what we will set out to do in ninety days.

First, you need to clean up the mess and do damage control, and it starts by owning the narrative. If you've had an issue at work or made a personal mistake, the best thing is to address it head-on with a genuine apology. Celebrities often acknowledge their mistakes with well-crafted PR statements. But before you record any disingenuous "apology" video for social media, put the gray hoodie and ukulele down and let's really plot here.

This is not about creating a fake apology just to appease people. Take the time to *actually* reflect on what happened and put in the work to understand the bigger issue. Self-reflection is uncomfortable but oh so necessary. No vague, "if I offended anyone" apologies. No defensive language. Instead, take accountability, understand why what you did was wrong, show growth, and emphasize a commitment to change.

Celebrity PR managers often tell their clients to stay off social media for a while after a public fallout. Could a "strategic silence" be exactly what you need right now? What would a break from social media mean for you? You don't need to announce it. Simply log out and stay logged out for a little bit. You'll be able to come back stronger once you've done the work on yourself. But before you log out, let's take some steps to control your digital footprint.

Audit your social media and delete any problematic or unprofessional posts that fuel a negative image of you. If you haven't cleaned up your chaotic social media presence in, well, since ever, then it's overdue. Clean up your LinkedIn, delete some photos, archive some Instagram photos, that sort of thing.

When I did my life rebrand after leaving Toronto at thirty years old, I took a much-needed look at my social media. It was obvious to me that it would take years to remove all my embarrassing drunk tweets, unprofessional photos, and rap freestyle videos. *Why did I insist on posting videos of myself freestyling on the Internet in the 2010s?! And so many of them?*

It was easier to just throw everything into the dumpster. So that's what I did. I deleted all my social media accounts and started fresh with all new profiles. But not before backing up all of my photos and videos to keep a record of all the fun for my personal collection. I'm not ashamed of my wild party girl days; it's just that the record of it is only for me now.

If you have anything on your social media that reflects a past version of you who isn't serving you now, delete it. Move on. Then, step away from social media for a month or two to reset the narrative.

During this strategic silence, consider staying off the radar in public, too. If you've had a falling out with colleagues, friends, an ex, or a former employer, don't gossip or overshare about the situation. Give it time. This is all part of a grand lifestyle shift, so while we're at it, why not cut ties with problematic people in your life, too? Stop spending time with people who bring you down. Network with those who inspire you instead.

Earlier in the book, I talked about how much our environment matters. Changing mine really helped. Think about upgrading your workspace. Redecorate your home, too. Also, spend time in new, positive places. Hint: this would be a good time to stop partying at dive bars and clubs in favor of being seen in the *right* places. I'm talking charity galas, art exhibitions, film festivals, and wellness retreats. Don't get me wrong, I love a good dive bar! I'm not saying to never go to a rowdy bar again. I'm only suggesting we take a break from that scene for a bit if your image could use polishing.

Scroll through your local events websites and register for a seat at a charity gala in your city. Put your classiest gown on and have fun schmoozing with a new crowd of people. If you see someone with a professional-looking camera, they might be press. Strike up a conversation and make sure you get photographed.

I bet you can tackle all of the above ideas in a month. Once that's worked out, start focusing on month two: curating your comeback. For this part, we need to take a real hard look at your brand story and get to work creating a new content strategy moving forward. It's time for your social reinvention!

After your strategic silence is over and you are ready to reemerge online, what now? What can you do to have a thoughtful media comeback? Well, obviously, promise yourself you'll avoid any more chaotic live streams, comment section arguments, or unhinged rants. You are above that now. This upgraded version of you would never, ever publicly react poorly in a negative manner. You are too classy for that kind of low-class behavior.

Instead, start posting about topics that align with the image you want to embody. This is how you reintroduce yourself! Through well-thought-out posts, polished visuals, intentional captions, and strategic partnerships. Personal branding matters! No matter if you're an entrepreneur, freelancer, a SAHM or corporate baddie, a strong online presence can change how people see you. You can control this by being mindful of what you post on social media. It also helps to have your own blog, where you can publish content that positions you as a thought leader and authority.

Earlier, I encouraged you to focus on being seen in the right places. Continue this! Attend industry events, social mixers, or pick up some new group hobbies. Can you get photographed with respected, scandal-free public figures? This can elevate your brand. Always be intentional about where you make appearances.

Next, we need to do a few things to take control of your name in the media. A public figure might schedule an exclusive interview with a trusted journalist. This lets them share their story and show their human side. It also helps them appear more self-aware. Your fall from grace could also benefit from a little positive media love! Consider pitching a story to your local newspaper.

I recommend taking some time to set up sit-down interviews, too. Focus on respected journalists, podcasters, and YouTube channels that match your new brand. If you've been meaning to do some charity work in your community, do it. Put your energy into the causes you care about, and align yourself with some positive press while doing good.

Celebrities who need some good press will plan staged paparazzi photo ops. This is so they can be photographed in "candid" moments of charity or good deeds. They'll let the photographers know where they are. This way, they can be snapped walking into a business meeting, volunteering, or giving $20 to a person in need.

You can do this too, even if you don't have paps following you around. You can pretend that you do. Think about photographers being everywhere you go. Imagine them taking photos the next time you enter a business meeting, leave a generous tip, or write a donation check. This visualization in your mind (if only for yourself) will get you into the flow of "yes, I am improving!" If you were perceived as unreliable, become someone people count on. If you have a reputation as someone with a bad attitude, start showing up with a positive mindset. Essentially, become the opposite of your bad press and show the universe that you are serious about leveling up.

Let's take it one step further. What if you were to go about your day-to-day life while pretending that you were on a reality TV show? That cameras and a production crew were following you around? You'd want them to capture you in your best light, right? Not only that, but you'd get to control the narrative, control the scene, say and do things to influence the other cast members around you. Well, real life is truly one big reality show, and you have free will. So why not put some energy into exemplifying this made-for-TV version of you now?

Also, in month two, put some focus on rebuilding your business or career. What new business ventures could you discover? A PR agent might suggest that you pivot into a new, fresh, profitable industry. Can you lean on your past scandal to launch yourself into a new project?

When Bravo star Stassi Schroeder found herself in hot water over bad behavior in 2020, she was publicly "canceled." Stassi took some time away from the spotlight to reflect on her mistakes and do some inner work. She came back a year or so later with a new book titled *Off With My Head*. The book detailed her fall from grace, her apology, and lessons learned. The book was named one of Us Weekly's Best Celebrity Memoirs of 2022 and became a New York Times bestseller.

Can you use your past missteps to tell your hero's journey? How about this for your new byline: "From reckless behavior to responsibly rich"? It's perfect for your finance book launch. Or your new mental health podcast could be, "From rock bottom to wellness coach of the stars." Not my best titles, but you get the idea.

Consider this your redemption project. You could start a professional blog, write LinkedIn articles, publish a memoir, begin a podcast, or mentor someone to show your growth. These types of media placements help you control the long-term narrative. If your work reputation is shaky, consider taking courses or getting certifications. You can also apply for new roles for a fresh start. And honey, get a mentor! Find someone who has been through similar struggles and seek their advice. People love a good comeback story and may be willing to help.

Now, let's move on to month three. The final stage of your PR emergency plan. This is where we build your money redemption arc and secure your bag. A celebrity would be advised to be selective with what roles she takes after a bad PR stint. Her comeback would be very controlled. Her agent would recommend that she say no to projects that could make her look desperate. Choosing to work with only the best and most aligned directors, producers, and companies instead. Getting a walk-on part in a favorite sitcom, joining a hit talk show, or performing unexpectedly at a major event can shift public perception. Then they'd work to get endorsements from some respected A-listers to co-sign some credibility and legitimacy for their comeback.

Not a celebrity? No A-list friends? No problem! You can still lean on this sentiment by diversifying your income. This means setting up new ways for money to reach you. So that you aren't depending on only one stream of income. Especially if your reputation has taken a hit in one industry. No better time than now to branch out into other things. Invest in businesses, real estate, and projects that will build long-term wealth. Open an Etsy shop, start freelancing, get into investing, monetize a blog, acquire an established business, just find a way to open lanes for money to reach you. The universe is trying to send money to you, so make it easier for her to do so.

Find a financial advisor who offers personalized advice. They will help you build wealth, pay off debts, and set up income streams that match your unique goals and situation. You will also want to be selective about opportunities. Much like a celebrity would decline a low-budget role that could make her look desperate, so should you. Don't jump at every job, client, sponsorship, or social invite. Try to align yourself with people, companies, and projects that reflect the new version of you.

Finally, if you were to take a step back and look at your financial situation, do you see room for improvement? Could you start budgeting better, paying off debt, and building an emergency fund?

When I started planning my financial future, building an emergency fund came first. Having that security of knowing that if anything unexpected happens, like if my car breaks down or there's some fee I have to cover out of the blue, I can. Don't overlook the importance of having an emergency fund.

Alright, now how do you feel about this whole mock-PR makeover exercise? Ready to face the public?

12

The Audacity to Be Content

What Happens When You Stop Chasing and Start Attracting

Ten years ago, if you'd told me that I'd be writing this book from a home I paid for with blog and digital products revenue, I would have thought you were joking given that, back then, I had no savings, no career, and no plan. My life was one revolving door of the same day on repeat, fighting for survival.

And now it's not. As I was grinding the beans for my coffee this morning in preparation for writing this final chapter, I found myself overcome with gratitude. Finally, I see that the best part of a lifestyle glow-up isn't the praise, accolades, or ability to buy more of what you want (although those things are fun). The best part is finally feeling safe in your own life and waking up without dread. And it's building something that gives you hope and joy. When that happens, you look around and realize you're living the life you used to fantasize about back when you'd doodle "crazy" goals on a notepad at your soul-crushing job to pass the time. (Could it be that you were manifesting this all along?)

This is what the result of your life glow-up can look like, too. It looks like knowing your finances are in check. It looks like walking past a mirror and thinking, "Wow, I look healthy!" It looks like setting boundaries with people who once made you feel small, no explanation needed. It looks like having a digital business that runs while you're offline enjoying life. It looks like *contentment*.

As I stood in my kitchen this morning, I realized I had been chasing this feeling of contentment all along. I know now that I don't want fame. I don't want my company to land on the Fortune 500 list. I don't want to manage a huge team or enterprise. What I *really* want is to continue to thrive as a solopreneur, earning income from the creative projects I enjoy while having all the time in the world to spend with my friends and family. And wouldn't you know it? I'm there.

My surroundings are filled with proof that my version of happiness is everywhere. The fridge is stocked with healthy food. I have a notepad filled with ideas for new content. I have an open calendar, to work when I please, so I never have to miss any of my son's soccer games. Next week, I'll be meeting up with Lana, Kylie, and Jane for a girl's weekend. I'm filled with love.

As I stirred my coffee, I glanced out the kitchen window and watched my son and dog run around the yard. I let a realization soak in. Contentment. Of course! That is true happiness, being content with what you have and where you're at, while knowing that everything is working out how it's supposed to. My house is a mess some days, my business goes through ups and downs some days, and that's totally fine. I'm oh-so grateful that I didn't end up selling Niche Investor. It's too good of a lead generator to let go, at least for now. *I love my life just how it is!*

Now, because I 'm a sucker for good word punnery, how funny is it that finding *contentment* for me was through creating *content*? I AM CONTENT has a double meaning. What it took to get here was, in a nutshell, believing that blogging could be a real career and then working to make it true.

It feels easy now, like the struggle is starting to be erased. Although, I'm sure it probably wasn't totally. Right? Wait a minute! I went from drop-shipping in a closet to closing six-figure deals, from couch surfing to owning a home. Can you hear the whirling sound of old tape spinning, as a little movie montage starts playing? There I was, standing at the side of the stage in the mall, a teenager, too terrified to step up to the mic to audition. Letting my fear block my opportunity. There I was again, post-grad, falling into one chaotic, unstable living situation and relationship situation again and again. Bawling my eyes out on the floor of the office I used to live in secretly, at my lowest point, feeling like everything was over. And the times, I'd briefly break out to find moments of peace—a moment appreciating the waves in solitude on Santa Monica Beach, another enjoying a solo coffee date— only to fall back into old habits for another round of the Allow Me to Eff This Up game.

It dawned on me that I didn't have to prove I wasn't the same broke, self-sabotaging, lost girl from a decade ago. I didn't have to fear that I'd slide back into my past like it was hovering above in a spaceship, waiting to abduct me. The fact was, I had built a new life. And it was stable.

In a full-circle moment, an email landed in my inbox from one of my coaching clients. She said:

> *"Chelsea, I cannot tell you how much your support, mentorship, and courses have helped and inspired me this year. I want to thank you for another incredible 1:1 call this week, and for all the ways you are helping to make my business a reality for me. Thank you from the bottom of my heart for helping me understand my business more and for making business FUN and aligned with who I am!"*

Staring at the kind words, I was overcome with emotion. It perfectly represents the fulfillment I find in helping other women and in using my platform for good,

Truthfully, I have spent years with a gnawing sense of urgency. Like stability was a life raft, and I was clinging to it with white knuckles, terrified it might drift away if I let go for even a second. I used to get so scared that I'd end up back where I started. Broke. Directionless. Living in an office. Drinking too much. Screwing up. Up until now, I'd dragged my past self along like a warning label, like a scarlet letter. Don't fall back and become her again, it warned. Because if I failed to succeed at my life goals, I'd be exiled right back into my past life of suffering.

Well, I don't believe that anymore. Today in my kitchen, feeling stable and calm, I realized that I'm not her anymore. And I don't need to be afraid of her. We are on to better things now, together.

Then I remember when the good habits started to stick. The time I deleted toxic people from my contacts. The first time I mapped out my Glow-Up Quadrants at thirty, finally choosing a new adventure. And how I declined an invite to Bottomless Margarita Night and instead opened my laptop to work on my blog. All part of the shift to nurturing creative pursuits, rather than wasting time in the clubs.

Now forty, I still create Glow-Up Quadrants. My goals and priorities may be different, but things like wealth and health are still in there. It's just that these days I'm also focused on other kinds of life stuff too, including hitting shared goals with Nick. We just completed our third house renovation, and we now run a successful home improvement blog and Youtube channel—a big leap from my days of squatting in an office building, eh? Life comes at you fast!

Clicking my heels like Dorothy I whisper, "there's no place like home." Of course, there are still challenges. There are bills to pay, algorithm shifts, and the pressure to keep all of the metaphorical plates spinning. Yet, those feel more manageable now.

I have the freedom to work from home as I please. I get to help other women do the same. I get to make little salads for the wild bunnies that live under the hedges on my property. *One day these bunnies will let me pet them!* I say to myself, determined as I stretch a handful of lettuce under the hedge. Knees in the dirt, butt in the air, and still dressed in my PJ's, my hair looking like I've been electrocuted. I am fully aware that the Amazon delivery driver assumes I'm a crazy person. But who isn't?

What do I now know for sure that I wish someone would have told me sooner? It's this. Believe in your creative ideas. Quit your job sooner. Start a blog sooner. Enter the creator economy sooner. Save and invest. Don't worry too much about boyfriends or dating. Focus on your wealth, health, education, and friendships. Oh, and try not to worry about looking cringe or trying to impress anyone. Yeah, I know that one is a toughie.

You've read the receipts, so you have seen me go from rock bottom to a fulfilling reality. I know it's possible for anyone, regardless of circumstance. I've been quasi-homeless, served wine I couldn't afford, and made a laundry list of mistakes, but I rebuilt my identity one decision and habit at a time. What changed wasn't the world around me; it was the way I started showing up in it. I learned how to glow up myself.

That means this isn't just my story. It can be a mirror of yours.

Your Turn

So here we are. You've made it this far. Through the late-night breakdowns, the caffeine-fueled ideas, the shadow work, the imposter syndrome spirals, and the accidental soul-searching that started this whole pursuit. Together, we've broken down the beliefs that were holding you back. You've acknowledged your cringey past, the messy middle, and have still chosen to show up.

Look at how far you've come. You've built tools, habits, systems, and, more importantly, self-trust. The hard part is done because you've sat with your shadow, looked your inner critic in the eye, showed up for yourself anyway, and decided to rewrite your story.

You now know how to make a plan, market your ideas, build a brand, sell with confidence, look the part, and cut out the self-trash talk. As you continue to glow up your life, you will face challenges and fight inner demons. Just remember, it's you who is in control. You get to design your version of fulfillment and success.

Even though you're now solidly identified with your future self, you don't need to be scared or embarrassed of your past self, either. Yes, the version of you who made mistakes, got into trouble, or let fear do the driving is not your enemy or some traitor you need to cast off the island like a bad contestant on a reality show. She got you here.

Every version of you that has existed up until this moment has been doing the best she could with what she had. Even if she fumbled, even if she lost her way, she survived. She kept going. And now, here you are, ready to step into the next era.

So, let's honor your past self. Appreciate her lessons, wisdom, and scars. Take a moment to send love back in time to her right now. How? Sit quietly and recall a difficult situation you experienced. Now, imagine that you are sending love energy to that past version of yourself. It sounds silly, but give it a try. Let her sit with you. In this safe, joyful, abundant life.

Really notice what you feel like after sending love energy back in time for just three minutes. By the way, you don't owe her an apology. You owe her proof that everything she went through wasn't for nothing.

If you ever feel lost again, return to the pages in this book. As, this book will remind you that "becoming your best self" is not some faraway object outside of you that you need to catch. Like it's a wild bunny you really want to pet and befriend but who's way faster than you and always just out of reach. No matter how many organic salads you put out. Your best self doesn't need catching because you are already her. Her nest just needed a bit of tidying, is all.

You have the tools to use for *any* reinvention. And remember to:

- Be your own safety net, hype woman, and boss.
- Stay focused on your *why* when doubt creeps in.
- Embrace change before life forces it on you.
- Forgive your past self so you can actually move forward.
- Ask for help when your brain says, You're on your own.

Thank you for choosing to spend your precious time with me. Time you could've spent doing literally anything else. You could've been scrolling, cleaning, zoning out to a true crime podcast, or taking a nap. Instead, you picked up this book, carved out a quiet moment, and walked through these pages with me. I'm honored! That means the world. I don't take it lightly that you let me into your mind, your energy, and maybe even your heart a little. I'm cheering for you louder than you know. If you want to share your thoughts and favorite takeaways from this book on social media, tag me @HerPaperRoute!

My greatest hope is that something here, a sentence, a story, a practice, stirs something in you. You've taken a leap into the next chapter of your life. And if you ask me, that's something worth celebrating. I hope you leave here feeling lighter and braver. I hope you've remembered who you are, and you're finally choosing her.

Always remember that no matter how chaotic your past may have been or how limited your resources are, you have the power to reinvent your life at any time. You have a say in your future. So take that leap. Start that project. Invest in that deal. Romanticize your morning routine. Raise your prices. Take up space. Hit publish. Reinvent. Send the pitch. *Sell the thing*.

Be the woman your past self didn't think was possible. Make her proud. It's a new beginning, babe. And I can't wait to see what you create.

With love, Chelsea Clarke :)

Wondering where to go from here? I got you! You don't have to figure it out alone. I invite you to join me and thousands of incredible women at HerPaperRoute.com. We're building businesses, rewriting stories, and celebrating wins. We also have classes and mentorship programs where I can work with you closely. If you're ready to take your next steps with support, strategy, and some serious momentum, come join our community.

Acknowledgments

Thank you to everyone who helped make this book happen. Big shout-out to my editor, Marie Timell, you are amazing. Thank you for your dedication to making this book great. Carole Edwards, Makenna Jacobs, Meagan Gunn, Heather Step, Jillian Bright and Jessica Jacobs, thank you for all your valuable feedback! To my photographer Camilla Topola, what would my branding be without you?

To my girl gang—Michelle, Allison, Lisa, Stormey, Alia, and Jessica, you've impacted and inspired me in this life more than you know. To my boys, Nick and Wolfe, and brother Eric, thank you for always seeing the humor in everything. Finally, thank you Mom for raising me to be independent and confident. And for teaching us the importance of being kind to all animals and insects. The world needs more people with your kind of empathy.